ŠKODA
OCTAVIA
THE FIRST ONE: 1959-1971
Miroslav Synek
The Story of a
Czechoslovakian
Automotive Icon

A VELOCE BOOK


Veloce is an imprint of David and Charles, Ltd
Email: info@veloce.co.uk | web: www.veloce.co.uk | tel: 01305 260068



First published in the UK and USA in 2026



A catalogue record for this book is available from the British Library.

ISBN-13: 9781836440406 paperback
ISBN-13: 9781836440987 ebook

Layout of the digital edition of this book may vary depending on reader hardware and display settings.

Printed in China by Asia Pacific Offset Group Ltd for:
David and Charles, Ltd
Suite A, Tourism House, Pynes Hill, Exeter, EX2 5WS

Veloce production team:
General Manager: Kevin Quinn
Commissioning Editor: Kizzy Taylor-Richelieu
Senior Book Editor: Becky Martin
Head of Design: Kevin Atkins
Production Manager: Sam Childs

# ŠKODA OCTAVIA

## THE FIRST ONE: 1959-1971

Miroslav Synek

The Story of a Czechoslovakian Automotive Icon

# CONTENTS

# FOREWORD

## Dear readers,

**WHAT MADE** me write my second book? It was, once again, my background, but also the desire to share an interesting story with you. I was born and brought up in Czechoslovakia, but I have been settled in the UK for a long time, and for the best part of my life I have been into old cars and aeroplanes. Škodas are probably the best known Czechoslovakian/Czech cars in the UK. I freely admit that I am biased: a 1960 Octavia was my parents' first car in, well ... 1960. I am a proud owner of exactly the same model (unfortunately, not the same car!).

However, other reasons for writing this book are more important. The modern day Octavia is a very good car, and is deservedly popular for its excellent build quality, space, reliability and economy. What many people do not realise is that there was an original Octavia back in 1959, just as good in its day as the modern one is today.

There is a widespread misconception that Škodas were rubbish until the company was bought by VW in 1991, but in reality they were great cars in the distant past before the long decline in the 1970s and 1980s. However, after joining the Volkswagen Group (Volkswagen AG) Škodas became very good cars *once again*.

The name Octavia is derived from Latin: it denotes Škoda's eighth small family car of the developmental line started by the Popular SV in 1934. The original Octavia was designed, built and further developed by highly competent, motivated designers, engineers and workers. They worked in Communist-ruled Czechoslovakia, often under very difficult circumstances. It is fair to say that the Octavia was the only Eastern European car of entirely indigenous design, fully competitive with its Western European counterparts in the small family car class. The Soviet Lada, also known as the VAZ 2101, and Romanian Dacia 1300 were good cars in their early form, but they were based on the Fiat 124 and Renault 12 respectively. The Octavia also laid the foundations for mass private car ownership in Czechoslovakia.

The Octavia was famous for its reliability and longevity, and those qualities came in handy when my friend Frank Anderson and I drove a 1962 Octavia Combi (estate) from Prague to Warsash near Southampton in 2012. We aimed to raise funds for an excellent nursery/pre-school supporting children with special needs in our local area. My other close friend, Steve Shrimpton, helped with the promotional campaign and, being very good with maps, also plotted our route before the trip. We were planning to avoid motorways and Steve did an excellent job plotting our route. However that well-laid plan went out of the window when we ran into major roadworks in Germany, which had begun earlier that same day. This would have held us up considerably but my great co-pilot Frank suggested: "Why don't we go down the motorway? The Old Girl is up to it!" Sure enough, she was!

When discussing the route before the drive, all three of us had underestimated the capabilities of the Octavia, which could in fact sustain acceptable motorway speeds for any length of time. Our drive was completely successful, and we raised significant funds for the pre-school from numerous donors and the sale of the Octavia to a local classic car enthusiast.

We then drove from Prague to Warsash in my 1960 saloon Octavia in 2016. This early Octavia needed more work prior to the trip as it had been laid up and not maintained for a number of years, but once sorted, this Old Girl also performed as an Octavia should.

Following the Russian invasion of Ukraine, my son-in-law's dad and I took the Octavia for a fundraising drive to support the British Red Cross' Ukraine Appeal. We drove from Warsash to Edinburgh and back, covering just under 1000 miles in total. The A68 from Darlington to Edinburgh, with its blind summits, sudden dips and sharp bends, requires some concentration, but the views it offers are breath-taking and, to me, it is the British answer to Route 66! The Octavia was also displayed (and attracted a great deal of interest) at the Scottish Italian Classics Day, an event held in Hopetoun House, a stately home near Edinburgh. I am very grateful to the organisers for allowing me to display my very non-Italian Octavia as part of fundraising to support Ukraine and its people. The Octavia performed faultlessly and we raised a considerable sum.

While writing this book, I relied mainly on Czech and Slovak sources, memories and experiences, including my own. The stories, facts and figures should be mostly correct, although human memory is imperfect. Different figures from various sources are provided in the book where appropriate, and when I am not sure about certain events or details, I will say so.

Enjoy!

**MIROSLAV ('MIREK') SYNEK**

## ACKNOWLEDGEMENTS

**MY HEARTFELT** thanks go to my friends Frank Anderson and Steve Shrimpton, to Marc Lawrence my other friend from the Solent Sky Museum, also to Mr Jiří Hulák from the Archive of the National Technical Museum in Prague and Mr Lukáš Nachtmann from the Škoda Archive in Mladá Boleslav. These gentlemen have given me many great ideas, comments and valuable pieces of information.

I am equally grateful to Mr Martin Plšek from Eurooldtimers Classic Car Club in the Czech Republic and Mr Zdeněk Patera running the www.auta5p.eu website for their permission to use the excellent photographs from their respective online galleries.

Finally, a big thank you goes to my wife Markéta and my whole family for their unfailing support.

*The majority of pictures have been reproduced from www.eurooldtimers.com or www.auta5p.eu unless stated otherwise.*

CHAPTER 1

# HISTORICAL CONTEXT

**THE OCTAVIA** was designed in the latter part of the 1950s, when the worst excesses of the Stalinist form of Communism were over in both the Soviet Union and Czechoslovakia. To offer better insight into that period I feel it would be helpful to go back some years before the design work started.

The Liberation from the Nazi occupation by Soviet and US forces in 1945 raised the hopes of all Czechoslovakians for freedom and eventual prosperity. The Red Army liberated over three quarters of Czechoslovakia, and suffered heavy casualties in the process, with well over 100,000 Soviet soldiers killed in action there. Sadly, many of the losses were preventable, and could have been significantly reduced by better tactics and closer co-ordination with the Czechoslovakian Resistance.

Understandably, there was a great deal of good will towards the Russians among Czechs and Slovaks after the war. This lasted until the Soviet occupation of the country in August 1968, whereupon it vanished literally overnight. The most frequently asked question by Czechoslovakians at that time was: 'We thought they were our friends. How could they do this to us?'

In fact, there were several reasons: the Communist Party of Czechoslovakia enjoyed a fair amount of popular support after the Liberation and was in a good position to seize power. The party claimed to have been the main force in the wartime Resistance, which was a highly debatable claim. Many individual Communists, mostly lower-ranking in the party hierarchy, did very well, showing courage and patriotism. Some successful Resistance groups consisted largely of Communists although many other Communists were sitting on their hands in the first critical years of the war until June 1941 when the Soviet Union was attacked. Prior to that date, the Soviet Union was an ally of Nazi Germany and Communists in occupied Europe were instructed not to take action against the Nazis.

Another reason why many Czechs and Slovaks supported the Communist Party was their disappointment with the West after the 1938 Munich crisis, when Nazi Germany was allowed to annex border areas of Czechoslovakia. The Communist Party's declared aim to reduce inequality and give better life prospects to the working class, and poorer people in general, was also completely legitimate and fair. What many people did not realise at the time was the enormous discrepancy between the Communist Party's words and actions. The party later came to be described as 'Saying something and doing the opposite'.

The take-over in February 1948 put the Communist leader Comrade Klement Gottwald in charge of the country. He quickly introduced a brutal dictatorship, in many ways similar to the Third Reich or Stalin's regime. The secret police, the StB (Státní Bezpečnost, Czech for State Security Police) was watching everyone and using methods comparable to those of the Gestapo. There were political show trials with fake charges, and more than 200 people were executed, with thousands more receiving long jail terms. In addition, TNP (Tábory Nucených Prací, Czech for Forced Labour Camps) were set up in October 1948. Like in the Nazi concentration camps, people who might have been opposed to the regime were 'preventively' detained in TNP without a trial, and although the number of detainees remains unclear, conservative estimates are between 20,000 and 30,000.

The social climate in Czechoslovakia became so oppressive that we cannot begin to imagine it today. This lasted until March 1953 when Klement Gottwald died at the age of 56, only days after Joseph Stalin, giving rise to speculation that he was disposed of by the Soviets who no longer needed him. However, such speculation is not supported by any evidence, and modern historic research suggests alcoholism and syphilis as likely causes. He was replaced by Comrade Antonín Zápotocký, who was less extreme but more dishonest. On 29 May 1953 he declared that rumours of an imminent currency reform were enemy propaganda. In fact new banknotes and coins had already been made in the Soviet Union(!) and transported to Czechoslovakia to be put into circulation on 1 June.

The reform destroyed people's savings as only a limited amount of money could be exchanged. The aim of the reform was to reduce the buying power of the population as the regime was unable to ensure adequate supply of consumer goods, and in that respect the reform succeeded completely. Officials of the Communist Party and State Security Police were given better exchange rates, which increased resentment even further. Widespread protests by workers were violently suppressed. However, the brutality of the regime then started to dwindle; political show trials ended, forced labour camps were closed, and detainees released by 1955. My parents and grandparents lived through those times, but my own experience is from the 1970s and 1980s. In my view the regime was no longer brutal by then, but it was massively dysfunctional and utterly corrupt.

The motor industry was re-organised and partly nationalized in late-1945. That in itself would not have been a problem. In fact, there was a comprehensive project of rebuilding the industry, referred to as The Czechoslovakian Project, and this 1947 proposal would have laid foundations for a truly modern, competitive car industry able to provide affordable cars of good quality for wide sections of the population. It was anticipated that the main car manufacturers such as Škoda, Praga and Tatra, as well as smaller companies like Aero and Jawa, would come forward with new designs, some already prepared secretly during the Nazi occupation of 1939-1945. Unfortunately, the Communist Party of Czechoslovakia was bitterly opposed to the project, and had it cancelled immediately after coming to power in February 1948.

The Communist take-over of the country resulted in complete nationalization of the industry but, more importantly, in incompetent individuals loyal to the party being appointed to leading positions. As in other industrial sectors, security was stepped up, ostensibly because of the risk of sabotage by 'reactionaries', but I suspect the real reason was to create a climate of fear. Armed security units referred to as Závodní Stráž (Czech for Factory Security) were set up, consisting of staunch Communists. The similarity with the Nazi Werkschutz is disturbingly close.

Private car ownership was seen as part of a 'bourgeois' lifestyle and frowned upon, and the priority was now lorries and military vehicles. However, implementation of full control by the Communist Party was relatively slow, and car production was rising steadily until 1950 when 24,463 cars were made. Then came a near-collapse and the figure for 1952 was 6295 cars. An alternative source indicates just 3553 cars made in 1952. Almost all were for the Communist Party, secret police or state-owned companies, with only 52 cars sold to private buyers that year. Yet another source suggests that figure was actually zero! As a result, Czechoslovakia no longer had an answer to anything produced by major European countries as had been the case before WW2.

The big U-turn came in summer 1953: the Communist Party decided that making cars available to the public would be a good thing after all. The possible reason was to remain faintly competitive with democratic countries in terms of standards of living. The by-then only remaining manufacturer of small cars, Škoda, was asked to design a car for large numbers of 'the working people' as the Communists referred to the population, and the result was the Škoda 440 Spartak; a decent small family car. This was replaced by the great Octavia in 1959, itself replaced in 1964 by the rear-engined Škoda 1000 MB, developed and built on a tight budget. However, production of the Octavia Combi (estate) continued until 1971, by which time the model was very outdated.

After the 1968 Soviet occupation of Czechoslovakia political purges followed. Investigation Committees were set up and those found to disagree with the 'Entry of Warsaw Pact forces' were sacked from their jobs. For the British reader this is, thankfully, an alien concept. To make it slightly more comprehensible, I would describe it as a version of McCarthyism on an industrial scale. The number of sacked is estimated at half a million-plus. The sacked became second class citizens. They were only allowed to do menial jobs regardless of their skills and qualifications, and their children had difficulties accessing higher education. The total population of Czechoslovakia was just under 15 million at that time, so the impact was huge. Unfortunately, the Škoda company was one of the hardest-hit. This resulted in the long decline in both design and build quality during the 1970s and 1980s. One particularly sad example was the Škoda 105/120 series, known as the Estelle in the UK. Older readers may still recall some of the numerous Škoda jokes:

**Q:** *How do you double the value of your Škoda?*
**A:** *Fill it up with petrol!*

However, even then there were many competent and dedicated designers, engineers and workers, often working against impossible odds, and it is thanks to them that some interesting prototypes were built. Unfortunately, their production was often blocked by the Communist Party. The successful Škoda Favorit launched in 1987 was also a result of their efforts. The new generation Octavia came along in 1996, seven years after the fall of Communism.

CHAPTER 2

# THE ANCESTRAL LINE

## ŠKODA POPULAR SV TYPE 906/7 (1934-1937)

**THE EARLIEST** version of the Popular became a game-changer, propelling the company to the position of the leading car manufacturer in Czechoslovakia. Production started in September 1934 in the main Škoda factory in the town of Mladá Boleslav, some 40 miles north-east of Prague.

In terms of performance, equipment and economy the Popular was comparable to other Czechoslovakian small family cars of the time, such as the Tatra 57 and Praga Baby. The British contemporaries in the same class included the Ford Model Y and Morris 8 Series I and II. The Popular was as fast as but more economical than the Ford, and very evenly matched with the Morris.

The straight-four, two-bearing engine of the SV was derived from the previous model Škoda 420 (the designation denoted four cylinders, 20bhp), but now produced 22bhp thanks to a higher compression ratio. The three-speed gearbox with synchromesh on second and third gears was also carried over from the 420. A new chassis with a central tube and transverse crossmembers for fixing the body, as first introduced in the 420, was strengthened without being made heavier. This became a characteristic feature of the whole developmental line of small family Škodas.

In contrast to older Škodas with beam-type axles, the Popular SV had fully independent suspension front and rear, making it the first Czechoslovakian car so-equipped. A differential was fitted as standard, and brakes were mechanical with drums on all four wheels. The Popular had rack-and-pinion steering, which was an advanced feature in 1934. Cars designated 906 were right-hand drive, those designated 907 left-hand drive (mainly for export, as Czechoslovakia was driving on the left until 1939).

*Škoda Popular SV 1935 in a period advert. (Courtesy Zdeněk Patera, www.auta5p.eu)*

The body still had a wooden frame (made of ash) covered with sheet metal, but its lines were elegant for the mid-1930s. There was a small luggage compartment was behind the rear seats, accessible from the inside, and the spare wheel was on the boot lid, covered by a smart fairing. There were two windscreen wipers fitted as standard. The Popular was a compact car with a low kerb weight which gave it good performance and economy for its day. The technical specification is summarised in Table 1.

TABLE 1

| Škoda Popular SV Type 906/907 (1934-1937) | |
|---|---|
| Length | 3770mm |
| Width | 1360mm |
| Height | 1500mm (saloon) |
| Wheelbase | 2430mm |
| Kerb weight | 750kg |
| Bore x stroke | 65x75mm |
| Capacity | 995cc |
| Power | 22bhp |
| Top speed | 56mph (90km/h) saloon, 62mph (100km/h) roadster |
| Acceleration | Not available |
| Average economy | 35-40mpg (7-8l/100km) |

Acceleration was described as much improved compared to the older Škodas, but I have not succeeded in finding exact figures (acceleration was rarely measured accurately in the mid-1930s). The fuel economy figure was achievable in mixed driving. The majority of early Populars were two-door saloons, and there were numerous convertibles. Four-door cars were also built, but they were rare, and there was a limited production of vans. The best-looking Populars were two-seater roadsters built in relatively small numbers.

In my view the roadsters are just as good-looking, if not quite as fast, as some superb British roadsters from the mid-1930s, such as the MG P-type or Singer Le Mans. Lighter than saloons or convertibles (*c*700kg kerb weight), roadsters were faster while retaining the same fuel economy. A two-door saloon was quite affordable at around 19,000 CZK and, interestingly, the rare roadsters were cheaper at 17,800 CZK. These prices were the equivalent of 15 to 17 average monthly salaries in the mid-1930s, making a Popular much more affordable than a Škoda 440 Spartak in the late 1950s (see Chapter 2).

Some Popular roadsters were fitted with more powerful 1386cc engines from the larger Rapid SV model. These could achieve 78mph (125km/h), which made them easily as fast as their British counterparts. One of these 'high-powered' Populars did well in the 1936 Rallye Monte-Carlo: the crew of Zdeněk Pohl and Jaroslav Hausman came second in the up to 1500cc class.

Production of the Popular SV reached 4220 cars before this version was replaced by the improved Popular OHV in early 1937. The significance of the Popular SV is that it paved the way for a succession of small family cars sharing a four-cylinder engine with rear-wheel drive, a central tube chassis and all-independent suspension. It also set high standards in terms of quality and reliability.

## ŠKODA POPULAR OHV TYPE 912 (1937-1938)

**THE SECOND** member of the developmental line was a major improvement on its predecessor, mainly because power increased to 27bhp from the same 995cc displacement. This made the Popular OHV faster – 62mph (100km/h) was now achieved by saloons and convertibles – while lighter roadsters came close to 69mph (110km/h). Fuel economy remained similar to the SV model, at 35-40mpg (7-8l/100km). Earliest cars built in the spring of 1937 had the same body as the Popular SV, but changes were soon phased-in.

The vast majority of Popular OHVs had a modernised, slightly wider body. While the length remained the same at 3770mm, the new body was 40mm wider at 1400mm. The radiator grille was now slightly convex, with a prominent perpendicular bar in the centre, the headlights were semi-integrated

*Very well-restored Škoda Popular SV roadster, a worthy competitor to the small, agile British roadsters of the period.*

into the wings and the boot was larger and accessible from the outside. The spare wheel was moved to the floor of the boot. The track was slightly wider and the wheelbase was marginally longer, which improved roadholding. The gearbox, steering and suspension remained unaltered.

The majority of Popular OHVs were two-door saloons with some four-door saloons, convertibles and roadsters also built. A small number were delivered as vans. Total production was 5510 cars by the spring of 1938 when the more powerful Popular 1100 OHV was introduced.

## ŠKODA POPULAR 1100 OHV TYPE 927 (1938-1939)

**THIS MODEL** introduced a completely new 1.1-litre engine, a straight-four like its predecessor, but wet cylinder liners made from chromium-nickel alloy were introduced, which improved cooling and extended the life of the engine. The crankshaft had three main bearings compared to two in the 995cc engines (both SV and OHV). The engine initially offered 30bhp and had great potential for improvement, with power considerably increased during its long development. Production of this engine was resumed after the Liberation in 1945 and modernised; more powerful versions were used in many post-war Škoda cars including the Octavia.

Reliability and longevity soon emerged as typical features of this engine. The gearbox remained the same, although four-speed gearboxes were gradually introduced with synchromesh on the top two gears. The rack-and-pinion steering and independent suspension were carried over from the earlier Populars, and hydraulic brakes were introduced on this model. Most cars had a body very similar to the later Popular OHV (Type 912), but the car was generally larger, more spacious and, inevitably, also heavier. Thanks to the more powerful engine, it was as fast as its predecessor in saloon or convertible guise. Roadsters were lighter, tipping the scales at some 840kg, and therefore faster. Fuel economy remained good, if marginally worse compared to the smaller-engined models. The 1100 OHV mainly competed with comparable

Czechoslovakian cars like the Praga Piccolo model of 1937 and Tatra 57B. It held its own well, mainly on account of its advanced engine.

The comparable British cars were Ford Model 7W and Morris 8 Series E, and they were evenly matched. The Vauxhall 10/4 was technically more advanced as it had an all-metal monocoque body. The majority of these Populars were two- or four-door saloons with an increased proportion of the latter, and total production until early 1939 was 6600 cars. Unlike previous Populars, the larger 1100 OHV was also built as an ambulance, in accordance with the Government policy of encouraging production of ambulances (and fire engines) because of the increasing threat posed by the Third Reich. The main technical data is given in Table 2.

**TABLE 2**

| Škoda Popular 1100 OHV Type 927 (1938-1939) | |
|---|---|
| Length | 3950mm |
| Width | 1480mm |
| Height | 1520mm (saloon) |
| Wheelbase | 2440mm |
| Kerb weight | 900kg |
| Bore x stroke | 68x75mm |
| Capacity | 1089cc |
| Power | 30bhp |
| Top speed | 62mph (100km/h) saloon, 69mph (110km/h) roadster |
| Acceleration | Not available |
| Average economy | 35-37mpg (7.5-8l/100km) |

*This picture of a Type 927 Popular OHV 1100 in the relatively rare convertible form shows the boot accessible from the outside. This car was restored extremely well, probably to better-than-new condition. There is some debate on the merits of restorations to concours standard, with differing schools of thought having valid points. While I admire the skills and effort put into such restorations, I personally prefer classic cars looking more period, in this case like a very well-maintained Popular Type 927 in about 1938. The Popular Type 912 OHV looked outwardly almost identical, but was noticeably smaller. White-walled tyres were not a standard feature at the time of production. (Courtesy Zdeněk Patera, www.auta5p.eu)*

*Popular SV Type 937 was one of the cheapest cars available in Czechoslovakia in 1938, but it was designed and built to a tight budget as exemplified by the single windscreen wiper.*

## ŠKODA POPULAR TYPE 937 (1938-1939)

**POPULARS WERE** becoming larger, heavier and more expensive (typical price for a Popular 1100 OHV was around 25,000 CZK). To counter this trend and keep the Popular affordable, Škoda introduced the simplified Type 937, also referred to as Liduška (pronounced *Lidushka*; interestingly, this is a diminutive of the Czech woman's name Ludmila).

The car was launched in mid-1938, and the model reverted to the old 995cc SV engine with 22bhp from the original 1934 Popular SV. It was much smaller than the 1100 OHV but performance and economy were the same as the earlier Popular.

In fact, the Type 937 harked back to the Popular's predecessor, the 420, as it had no differential and only one windscreen wiper was fitted. However, the Type 937 had *both* the trafficators and indicator lights, like the far more advanced Type 938. Technically, this 'budget' model represented a major retrograde step, but it was inexpensive: typical price for a two-door saloon (the most common version) was 17,300 CZK. Production was 1519 cars, including some ambulances built on the orders of the Nazi occupiers during the war, and small numbers of cars were assembled just after the Liberation.

In my childhood in the 1960s Populars of various versions were among the most common pre-war cars, with many thousands of them still on the road. They were reliable, long-lived cars giving good service to many families. I recall liking them, but thinking they were too common compared to, say Aeros or Walters!

## ŠKODA POPULAR 1100 OHV TYPE 938 (1938-C1942)

**THE TYPE** 938 was technically similar to the Type 927, except for a marginally more powerful engine offering 32bhp from the same 1089cc capacity. The body was very different, however; much more rounded in shape and with horizontal bars for the grille. The Type 938 was also larger at 4050mm long and 1500mm wide. The wheelbase was further increased to 2480mm, and the track was also wider than before. The Type 938 introduced indicator lights, but still retained trafficators, and, somewhat surprisingly, running boards were re-introduced. As Czechoslovakia was planning to convert to driving on the right, the Type 938s were left-hand drive, in contrast to the majority of older Populars. Another difference was the bonnet hinged on its trailing edge and opening upwards rather than two halves opening sideways. Performance and economy were similar to the Type 927, but the Type 938 was slightly more spacious.

Production of mainly two-door saloons and some convertibles started in the autumn of 1938 and continued slowly during much of the Nazi occupation, with the cars taken over by the occupiers. Small numbers were also built after the war. Total production was 1019 cars. The Type 938 was a very modern small family car by the standards of the late 1930s, and while it still had a body with a wooden frame, it was so advanced that it could be only slightly updated after WW2 and built as the Škoda 1101/1102 Tudor.

*Well-restored, rare Škoda Popular 1100 OHV (Type 938) saloon at a classic car show in the Czech Republic. This was the best Popular of them all, but sadly emerged at the worst possible time, just a few months before the Nazi occupation.*

*Škoda 1101 Tudor in the most common two-door saloon version.*

## ŠKODA 1101 AND 1102 TUDOR TYPE 938 (1946-1952)

**THE FACTORY** in Mladá Boleslav was severely damaged by an air raid on 9 May 1945, and there is still some debate as to which air force was responsible. This happened just after the German surrender, and the Luftwaffe was in no position to assemble a force of bombers and launch a raid. The prevailing view of modern Czech historians is that the raid resulted from navigational errors by the Soviet Air Force. When Germany surrendered on 7 May 1945, one of the surrender terms was that all German units would stay in their present positions and wait to be captured by Allied forces. Some German units due to be captured by the Soviets attempted to move away as they preferred to be captured by the US forces, putting them in breach of the surrender terms. The Soviets wanted to stop these German units and launched bombing raids.

The attacks were completely legitimate, but the navigational error had tragic consequences including more than 100 Czech civilians killed. The damage to the factory was extensive, but rebuilding the plant was a priority and the authorities could rely on popular support. Most of the damage was repaired before the winter of 1945 and the factory resumed limited production in the autumn, mainly focussing on design and production of the new Škoda 1101, which was basically the pre-war Popular 1100 OHV Type 938 with a more modern body. The 1101 was of a more rounded shape and, in contrast to its predecessor, had no running boards.

Tudor is not an official name; it is a Czech form of two-door referring to the fact that the majority of 1101s and 1102s were delivered as two-door saloons. This new small family car went into production in mid-1946 and, as it shared many components with its predecessor, the Popular Type 938, the type number was left unchanged.

*Well-restored and very rare Škoda 1102 roadster.*

*Rare four-door Škoda 1102 Tudor. 'Four-door Tudor' sounds faintly absurd, but that's how it was described in my old country! Five thicker transverse decorative bars on the radiator grille are noticeable, otherwise it is hard to tell the difference from the Škoda 1101. The pictured car was used by Czechoslovakian Embassy in Belgrade (then Yugoslavia) in the early 1950s.*

The chassis was identical, with the central tube, crossmembers for fitting the body and independent suspension front and rear, typical of Škodas. There were transverse leaf springs front and rear and lever arm shock absorbers. A differential was standard, as on the vast majority of Populars, but steering was now by screw-and-nut which was a retrograde step.

The engine was the well-proven OHV four-cylinder of 1089cc capacity, brakes were hydraulic and the four-speed gearbox with floor change had synchromesh on third and fourth gears. The body was more modern compared to the Popular Type 938, but still with a supporting ash frame. Like its predecessors, the Tudor was well built and reliable. Its main asset was the tough engine with good development potential and capable of high mileages. I have read claims that these engines could have up to four rebuilds, each after some 100,000 miles (160,000km). Technical details are summarised in Table 3.

TABLE 3

| Škoda 1101/1102 Tudor Type 938 (1946-1952) | |
|---|---|
| Length | 4050mm |
| Width | 1500mm |
| Height | 1520mm (saloon) |
| Wheelbase | 2485mm |
| Kerb weight | 940kg |
| Bore x stroke | 68x75mm |
| Capacity | 1089cc |
| Power | 32bhp |
| Top speed | 62mph (100km/h) saloon, 66mph (105km/h) roadster |
| Acceleration | Not available |
| Average economy | 33-35mpg (8-8.5l/100km) |

The 1101 was mostly built as a two-door saloon, but there were some four-door saloons, two-door convertibles, estates, vans and even ambulances. Very few were built as two-seater roadsters, and they were mainly for export; these were very good looking but too slow to make convincing sports cars. Production continued until 1949, when the Škoda 1102 was phased-in, this version differing just in minor details such as a slightly different radiator grille with thicker and less numerous horizontal decorative bars.

The only major, and controversial, difference was a column gear change introduced in the 1102. This was very fashionable from the late 1940s until the early 1960s, but made driving less easy and potentially complicated maintenance. The Tudor remained in production until summer 1952. Production was 66,904 cars, substantially more than production runs of various versions of the Popular, and the total was roughly equally divided between 1101 and 1102 versions.

Tudors were not really perceived as old cars in my childhood, as the later production ones were only about 10 years old. They are now quite popular classics in the Czech Republic and Slovakia. To my knowledge, there is limited secondary production of spare parts in the Czech Republic.

## ŠKODA 1101 TUDOR VO (1948-1951)

**THIS WAS** a version of the Tudor built for the military and police as a staff or rapid response car, and VO stands for Vojenský Osobní (Czech for military car). The engine, gearbox and chassis were identical to the standard Tudor 1101, so the VO was rear-wheel drive. Even ground clearance was not significantly higher compared to its civilian counterpart and it had a completely different, angular body with fabric roof and detachable side

*1101 VO was colloquially referred to as 'bojový Tudor' (Czech for fighting Tudor). Realistically, not much of a fighter though ...*

windows. That body gave it a very military appearance, but, with no off-road capability, the reality was rather different. Dimensions were similar to the civilian model, but the 1101 VO was significantly heavier at 1040kg and, as a result, it was slower with a top speed around 56mph (90km/h). Fuel economy also suffered, the 1101 VO typically returning some 28mpg (10l/100km). The model was in production from 1948 to late 1951 and 4237 cars were built. Many were sold as army surplus to private owners in the 1960s, which is why I thought I should describe it here. Small numbers are still in the possession of Czech and Slovak classic car enthusiasts today.

## ŠKODA 440 SPARTAK TYPE 970 (1955-1959)

**AS WITH** the Tudor, Spartak is not an official name but everyone was using it when discussing these cars. The designation 440 denotes four cylinders and 40bhp. This immediate predecessor of the Octavia was a result of the U-turn on private car ownership in the highest circles of the Communist Party. Until 1953 the prevailing view was that car ownership was part of a 'bourgeois' lifestyle and as such should be actively discouraged, but after the deaths of Joseph Stalin and Klement Gottwald, slightly less extreme Communists reached the leading positions in both the Soviet Union and Czechoslovakia. It was recognised that, to retain some of its vanishing credibility, the regime needed to be at least remotely competitive with democratic countries in terms of living standards.

Part of this drive was a new emphasis on making car ownership more accessible to wider sections of 'the working people', which

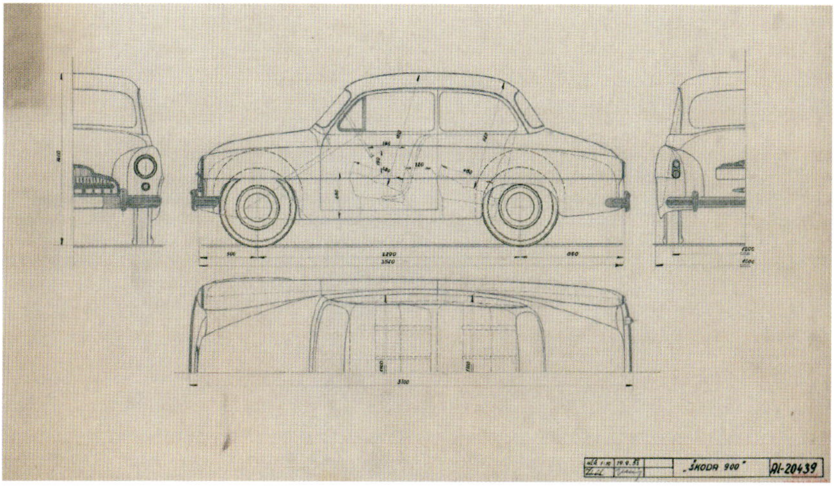


*Škoda 900 design No 1 was much smaller than the final Spartak prototype but of similar shape. Design No 2 was little different. (Courtesy Škoda archive, Mladá Boleslav, Czech Republic)*

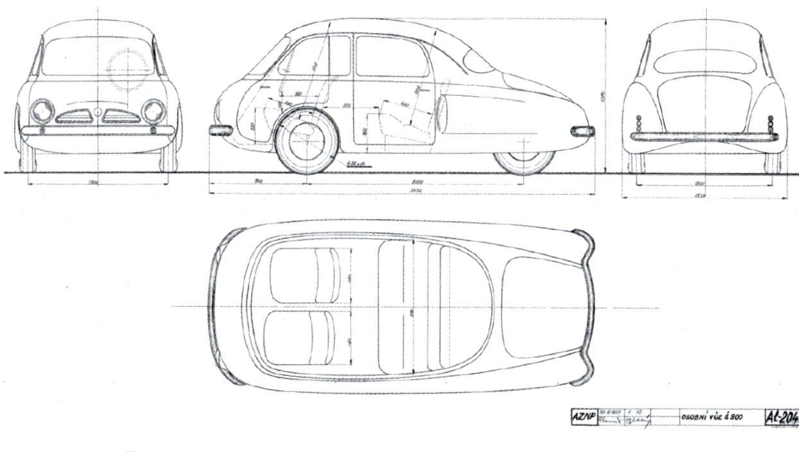


*Rear-engined Škoda 900 design No 3 was completely different from No 1 and No 2, in fact rather reminiscent of microcars common in the 1950s. (Courtesy Škoda archive, Mladá Boleslav, Czech Republic)*

was the standard Communist term for the population. By that point Škoda was the only Czechoslovakian car manufacturer of any significance (Tatra, the producer of brilliant streamlined, rear-engined cars was ordered to make only lorries and military vehicles in 1952). The Škoda company, now officially re-named AZNP (Automobilové Závody Národní Podnik, Czech for Nationalized Car Factory) was therefore asked to design an affordable 'people's car'.

Preliminary studies were begun in summer 1953, and it was clear from the very start that the best way forward would be a small family saloon. Three design studies were ready for detailed evaluation by September 1953, and they were designated Škoda 900, the number denoting the capacity of a small engine yet to be developed. Designs No 1 and No 2 were small, fairly orthodox two-door saloons with the engine in front and rear-wheel drive. The main difference was that No 1 had a more rounded shape both front and rear, while No 2 was more angular, but their dimensions were very similar.

Both versions shared a short wheelbase of 2200mm and a track of 1200mm front and rear. No 1 was 3720mm long, 1500mm wide and 1370mm tall while No 2 was marginally shorter at 3700mm and taller at 1400mm but width was the same. Design No 3 was radically different: the engine was in the rear, driving the rear wheels. The overall layout was faintly reminiscent of the later Fiat 600 Multipla, although the Škoda design had only two doors, and the BMW Isetta also bore some resemblance. The wheelbase was very short at 2000mm, the track in front was 1300mm, 100mm wider than in No 1 and No 2. The track at the rear was the same as in the other two studies at 1200mm, although this design was considerably shorter overall at 3550mm.

All three designs were to be four-seaters, although very 'cosy' even by the standards of the early 1950s. Interestingly, No 3 was slightly more spacious in the rear, offering 1200mm of internal width to rear-seat passengers compared to 1100mm of the other two designs. No 1 and No 2 also offered 1100mm of internal width to front-seat passengers, the corresponding figure not available for No 3. None of the three designs progressed beyond the drawing board stage.

*Škoda 990, the first prototype of the Spartak as completed on 19 December 1953. This prototype still had a wooden frame, and the petrol tank in the engine compartment. (Courtesy Zdeněk Patera, www.auta5p.eu)*

It was recognised that developing the new car from scratch including its 900cc engine would take too long. The key meeting that decided further direction was chaired by Mr Stanislav Císař, the Managing Director of the AZNP (the new name of Škoda) on 7 October 1953. The meeting was attended by senior figures of the company, including Mr František Přibyl the Chief Designer, Mr Karel Hrabánek the Chief Engineer, Mr Václav Medek responsible for planning, Mr Josef Velebný leading the bodywork design and several others.

The decision was made to design a slightly larger car, using as many components as possible from the existing models, mainly the 1101/1102. The design team was given an absurdly short deadline, the new prototype to be designed and built by 19 December 1953 to celebrate the birthday of the Czechoslovakian president, Comrade Zápotocký. In a nutshell, the Communist Party that was still totally opposed to private car ownership in the spring of 1953 was now asking the designers, engineers and workers to produce a small family car within two months!

The Škoda workforce involved in the new project was working extremely long hours including weekends throughout the rest of October, the whole of November and right up to 19 December, 1953. A wooden model in 1:10 scale was built, followed by the first fully functional prototype. The prototype was indeed completed at 4am on that very day! It was initially referred to as Škoda 990, but the unofficial name Spartak soon caught on, and, before too long, the new model was

*This picture of the first prototype shows the layout of the boot with the long boot lid reaching to the rear bumper. Unfortunately, this practical feature had to be abandoned because of inadequate structural strength. The rear lights are much smaller than on production cars. (Courtesy Zdeněk Patera, www.auta5p.eu)*

referred to as Spartak 990. The car was due to be presented to the high-ranking officials of the Communist Party and Ministry of Industry. However, the Comrades were apparently too busy and the presentation could only take place on 21 December 1953. It is worth describing this first of all Spartaks in detail. The technical specification is given in Table 4.

The car was larger then the three design studies. The engine was the well-proven straight-four OHV unit, but with bore reduced from 68mm to 65mm and the 75mm stroke retained this gave the capacity of 995cc. The engine was relatively high-revving, offering its maximum output of 31bhp at 4500rpm. The power was 1bhp less than the 1089cc version in the Popular 938 of 1938 and post-war Škoda 1101/1102 Tudor, both described earlier in this chapter. The four-speed gearbox was carried over from the larger Škoda 1200 Sedan – a

TABLE 4

| Škoda 990 Spartak prototype (1953) | |
|---|---|
| Length | 4000mm |
| Width | 1600mm |
| Height | 1420mm |
| Wheelbase | 2400mm |
| Kerb weight | 932kg |
| Bore x stroke | 65x75mm |
| Capacity | 995cc |
| Power | 31bhp |
| Top speed | c62mph (100km/h). See text for more details |
| Acceleration | 0-50mph (0-80km/h) 26-30 seconds. See text for more details |
| Average economy | 34mpg (8.2l/100km) |

four-door saloon mainly manufactured for the offices of the Communist Party, State Security Police and state-owned companies – and had synchromesh on third and fourth gears. The Spartak 990 retained the all-independent suspension of previous Škodas, with transverse leaf springs front and rear, and the suspension and many other components including hydraulic drum brakes were carried over from the 1101/1102 Tudor, as was the screw-and-nut steering. In total, some 75% of components were identical.

However, the two-door body of a pontoon type was completely different and much more modern. The internal space was considerably improved compared to the three original design studies, and four adults could be carried in relative comfort. The dashboard was symmetrical, with a cluster of three dials on the left (in front of the driver) and an open storage space for small items on the right. The dials included a fuel gauge, speedometer calibrated to 120km/h (75mph) and coolant temperature indicator.

The prototype had a reasonably sized boot with the spare wheel on its floor, but in contrast to production cars the boot lid reached to the rear bumper, which made loading easy. Unfortunately, this gave inadequate strength to the rear part of the body and production cars required a much shorter boot lid. The kerb weight was relatively high at 932kg, the likely reason being the prototype still had a body with a wooden frame, and the maximum useful load capacity was 350kg.

With just 31bhp on tap, the Spartak 990 was distinctly underpowered and hard pushed to achieve a 62mph (100km/h) top speed. I have been able to find some results of the early test drives from January 1954 onwards. With shorter constant ratio of 5.25:1 the prototype achieved a top speed of just under 60mph (95.5km/h), a figure typically associated with small family cars in the mid-1930s. The 0-50mph (0-80km/h) 'sprint' took 26 seconds. A longer final drive ratio of 4.78:1 was also tested and the top speed increased to 65mph (104km/h) but the acceleration worsened further, and 50mph (80km/h) could now be achieved in 30.5 seconds from standstill. Fuel economy was described as better in the latter configuration for which I found the accurate figures, the Spartak 990 returning just over 42mpg (6.6l/100km) at an average of 37.5mph (60km/h). In faster driving with an average of 50mph (80km/h) the fuel economy worsened to just over 34mpg (8.2l/100km).

The first prototype was followed by a batch of 25 progressively more modified prototypes, these built in the early months of 1954. Some were retained by the factory for further testing, but the majority were offered for use as 'company cars' to various important institutions: the Central Committee of the Communist Party of Czechoslovakia, the Town Committee of the Communist Party in Mladá Boleslav, the Office of Czechoslovakian Government and various Ministries. Even the Office of the President of Czechoslovakia was offered two prototypes. This seems strange by today's standards, but the circumstances were very different in Communist Czechoslovakia; it was essential to impress the high-ranking Comrades ... and to be in their good books.

There was ever present worry among the designers, engineers and workers that the Communist Party might kill off the whole project. Fortunately, this did not happen as the Comrades were sufficiently impressed, and it also helped that one of the prototypes was shown to the public at the 'May Day Rally of the Working People' on 1 May 1954. This was an annual parade organised by the regime and the attendance was 'recommended'. I freely admit that my wife Markéta and I took some time to work out the most accurate English expression, but we then succeeded with the help of my friend Steve, who has, among other talents, a great understanding of Czechoslovakian history and culture.

In the meantime, the Škoda team

continued their hard work. It was recognised that the prototypes with the smaller 995cc engine were severely underpowered. Twenty still had the smaller engine, but the last five received the standard 1089cc unit, initially tuned to 37bhp. One of these later cars was performance tested in June 1954 and top speed improved modestly to 67mph (107.5km/h), but acceleration was now much better: 0-50mph (0-80km/h) took 22.6 seconds. In fact, fuel economy also improved, with 34mpg (8.2l/100km) now returned at an average speed of 54mph (86km/h). Further improvements included placing the 30-litre fuel tank under the right (off-side in the UK) rear wing, away from the engine bay, and this was a significant safety feature, reducing the risk of fire in case of an accident. It was also recognised that the wooden frame would hamper mass production.

The Communist Party and Government approved production on 20 July 1954. Škoda then built three final prototypes, referred to as 'final model' with designation Škoda 970 (yes, I know it is illogical after the wooden-frame prototypes designated Škoda 990). These had an all-metal body attached to the separate chassis, and the boot lid was shortened to give better structural strength. They also had a different, asymmetrical dashboard with a lockable storage compartment on the front passenger side.

The final prototypes had a speedometer calibrated to 140km/h (88mph), just like production cars, and an ashtray in the centre of the dashboard was another new feature. One of the final prototypes was named Orlík (Czech for young eagle), and exhibited at the Brussels Motor Show in January 1955. It carried a Škoda inscription (AZNP was largely unknown) with number 1100 denoting engine capacity. However, to keep the Comrades happy, a globe with the inscription AZNP was in the hub of the decorative 'propeller' in front of the radiator grille. The Orlík had small position/safety lights on the B-pillars just under the roof. This elegant feature was abandoned on production cars and only re-introduced in late production Octavias in 1963.

The response of the Belgian public and international motoring press was positive, the new Škoda attracting much interest. This model had a 1089cc engine tuned to 41.5bhp at 4250rpm and maximum torque was 74Nm, the power and torque marginally more than in production cars and even the earliest Octavias. Unfortunately, performance was somewhat blunted by excessive weight, which at 991kg was the highest of the whole Spartak/Octavia development line. As a result, the car was slow, only achieving just over a 66mph (106km/h) top speed, which did not compare well with one of the other (lighter) final prototypes that had achieved 70mph (112km/h).

After the Brussels Motor Show, discussions took place in February 1955 about the final name of the new model. The name Spartak could not become official because of concerns about possible legal problems with a Dutch motorbike maker of the similar-sounding Sparta, and the alternatives such as Orlík or Rival did not find much favour. In the end, it was decided to name the car Škoda 440, the designation denoting four cylinders, 40bhp. However, the official name never really caught on and most Czechoslovakians referred to the car as the Spartak; indeed, the earliest production cars bore the inscription Spartak on the bonnet just above the radiator grille, but this was soon discontinued.

The new Škoda (almost no one was using the somewhat vague abbreviation AZNP) was introduced to the Czechoslovakian public by the motoring journal *Svět motorů* (Czech for *World of Motoring*) in early August 1955. Production had started shortly beforehand, and first production cars became available in late October 1955. Prior to its launch on the Czechoslovakian 'market' (the reason for the quotation marks will become obvious after reading the next few pages), the Spartak was shown at the Frankfurt am Main International Car Show and the London Motor Show. The response was just as positive as it had been in Brussels in January of the same year. For reasons unknown, the Spartak was not shown at the equally important Paris Motor Show, but the domestic Brno Motor and Engineering Show in the largest city of Moravia was not short-changed and a Spartak was presented there.

Production Spartaks had the well-proven 1089cc engine, the same as the final prototypes. The engine now had a light alloy block and offered 40bhp and torque was 69Nm. Development potential was one of the advantages of this engine, as was reliability and longevity. The electrical system was now 12V. The gearbox had four speeds, initially with synchromesh on third and fourth gears, although later cars built from March 1957 also had synchromesh on second. Production Spartaks had independent suspension front and rear with transverse semi-elliptical leaf springs, retained screw-and-nut steering, and drum brakes were hydraulic.

The separate chassis was typical Škoda, with a central tube branching in front to accommodate the engine. There were two crossmembers carrying the all-metal body, and the Spartak was the first Škoda with indicator lights and no trafficators. All 440s were two-door saloons. Interestingly, design studies of an estate version were completed in summer 1955, but did not progress any further. Spartaks were compact but quite spacious, with a boot of decent size (300-litre volume) and the spare wheel was now held by a cradle fixed to the front part of the boot. Technical specification of the standard production Spartak is given in Table 5.

The Spartak weighed 920kg, which made it considerably lighter than the Orlík prototype, so the official top speed could realistically be achieved. Cruising speed was 50-56mph (80-90km/h) and the Spartak was also quite economical as well as being well built and generally reliable. However, there were problems with the quality of various materials and components. This particularly applied to the alloys used for engine production, metal sheets for making bodies, leaf springs, chromed bumpers and decorative propellers, while other low-quality parts were windscreens (in some cases so poor that they cracked spontaneously) and interior trim. This caused numerous well-justified complaints and warranty claims, and I have found the figure of 4,500,000 CZK paid out by Škoda in warranty claims in 1958 alone. Given the number of cars produced in that year (see later) the statistical average is just over 130 CZK per car, not a negligible sum of money in 1958 Czechoslovakia.

It must be considered that the Škoda factory and its various sub-contractors were state-owned companies totally dependent on funding from the state. The funding was inadequate and corners had to be cut. First production cars from October 1955 were also poorly equipped: they only had one wiper, no heater and no telescopic shock absorbers at the rear. This caused much dissatisfaction even in the severely under-

**TABLE 5**

| Table 5: Škoda 440 Spartak Type 970 (1955-1959) | |
|---|---|
| Length | 4065mm |
| Width | 1600mm |
| Height | 1430mm |
| Wheelbase | 2400mm |
| Kerb weight | 920kg |
| Bore x stroke | 68x75mm |
| Capacity | 1089cc |
| Power | 40bhp at 4200rpm |
| Compression ratio | 6.8:1 |
| Top speed | 69mph (110km/h) |
| Acceleration | 0-50mph (0-80km/h) c22 seconds, 0-62mph (0-100km/h) probably c32 seconds |
| Average economy | 37mpg (7.6l/100km) |

*Škoda 440 Spartak with two-tone paint and tyres with white sidewalls indicating that this is an export version. Cars for the domestic market were much more austere.*

*Typical dashboard of a production Spartak probably built after March 1957 when column gear change became standard. Features worth noting include the umbrella-shaped handbrake handle just left of the steering column and the small closed storage space on the right-hand side of the dashboard. The small cream button left of the handbrake handle is for operating the cable releasing the bonnet latch.*

*Well-restored Škoda 440 Spartak as it was sold in Czechoslovakia. Chrome bumpers and headlight bezels suggest that this car was built after March 1957 when the Standard version was phased out. The fog lights and external mirror are after-market, they were never standard. Unlike on Octavias the wheel rims were often colour-coded with the body on Spartaks.*

supplied Czechoslovakian car market, but from November 1955 onwards all cars had a heater, two wipers and telescopic rear shock absorbers, and these items were retro-fitted to the earliest cars free of charge. Production was initially very slow, with only 1000 cars built between October 1955 and the end of the year. The production figures increased considerably from 1956 onwards, the best year being 1958. This was the last full year of Spartak production, and 34,479 were made by the end of the year.

From the very start of production, the Spartak was exported in substantial numbers that exceeded half of all those built. Destinations included many European countries: Austria, Belgium (where they were also assembled), Finland (the largest importer), France, Germany (West), Holland, Norway, Sweden and the UK. One 440 was displayed at the Earls Court Motor Show in 1956 and attracted much interest. The Spartak was selling quite well as it was reliable and economical, and the UK price of £841 7s (including Purchase Tax) was average for a small family car in 1957. Spartaks were also delivered to Eastern European countries including East Germany, Hungary and Poland and smaller numbers were exported to exotic locations such as Australia and New Zealand. More Spartaks (about 1100 including 100+ more powerful 445 models) were exported to the United States, where they were moderately popular as second cars and, interestingly, these cars were fitted with air-conditioning from May 1958.

From the start of production until March 1957 there were two versions of the Spartak: the Standard was for the domestic market, the Export for ... well ... export, and their level of equipment was different. While the

Standard had painted bumpers (colour-coded in today's terminology) the Export had chromed items as well as chromed sideskirts. The Standard had only one sunvisor, in the Export there were sunvisors for the driver and front passenger, and the Export was often delivered in two-tone paint which made it look very smart. Technically, the main difference was that the Standard had a floor gear change with the lever atop the central tunnel, while the Export had the fashionable but less practical column gear change.

From March 1957 all models were built in the Export version bar two-tone paint which was now optional, in theory available also on the domestic market. Development of the Spartak during its production run was relatively limited. Early production cars had wheel rims with multiple semi-circular cut-outs around the inner circumference, colloquially referred to as 'kopretiny' (Czech for daisies!) but cars built from summer 1958 onwards had wheel rims with narrow-slit cut-outs like the later Octavias. All production cars were fitted with 15-inch wheels, while some prototypes had 14-inch items.

The extensive export of Spartaks brought the desperately needed hard currency to the regime's coffers, but had a major downside: inadequate supply for the domestic market. The majority of car owners in Czechoslovakia still had pre-war cars in the mid-1950s, and the artificially induced collapse of car production in the early 1950s had created a significant gap. While production of the Spartak was achieving decent annual figures, it was not nearly adequate and the market was very under-supplied. The Communist Party decided to regulate the market, and I thought it would be helpful to describe the system in some detail. The price was set arbitrarily at 27,450 CZK by the Ministry of Industry, regardless of production expenses let alone profit, and this made the Spartak expensive. As the average monthly salary was around 1200 CZK, the Spartak could be purchased for some 23 average monthly salaries.

It has to be considered that most people had very little in the way of savings after the 1953 currency reform. The price was increased to 28,590 CZK, an equivalent of nearly 24 average monthly salaries, in March 1957. That made the Spartak even less affordable, but finding the money was not the only problem prospective buyers were facing as cars were only available to those in possession of the Car Purchase Permit (another translation I had to work out with my friends Frank and Steve!). The line taken by the Communist Party was that the permission to buy a car should be a reward for citizens contributing to 'building Communism' in an extraordinary way.

Anyone could apply for the Permit, but the majority were turned down at an early stage of the complex application process; the application had to be supported by references from the unified (Communist-controlled) trade union, the branch of the Communist Party from the applicant's workplace and the local branch at his/her address. The applicant's line manager also had a say ... as had his or her bank! Confirmation of no outstanding debts was required, rather like good credit rating today. Getting the worst of both worlds is the expression springing to my mind ... or is it just me?

In addition, the applicants had to declare in writing that neither they nor their spouses already had a car. Finally, they had to confirm that if they sell the car in the first two years of ownership, they would have to sell it to the Mototechna (state-owned car dealership) for the official price set by the dealership. When the lucky prospective buyer completed all these forms and passed all the hurdles, the next step was paying the deposit of 20,000 CZK. After that, the Car Purchase Permit holder was waiting to be notified of a car becoming available. It was 'a car', there was no question of choosing colour let alone optional equipment. When the Permit holder was notified, the car had to be collected and the balance paid within two weeks; if it was not collected it was offered to the next Permit holder on the waiting list. The whole system was open to corruption and abuse of position, both of which were widespread. Total production of the Škoda 440 Spartak was 75,417 cars built until January 1959.

## ŠKODA 445 SPARTAK TYPE 983 (1957-1959)

**THIS WAS** a slightly more powerful model with a 1221cc engine, identical to that of the larger model Škoda 1201 Sedan, which was a more powerful successor to the Škoda 1200 Sedan. These four-door Škodas represented a different development line and they are described in my book, *Cars from my Old Country*. The power was 45bhp, but torque reached 84Nm, quite a significant improvement over the 1089cc engine. According to the official figures top speed was 72mph (115km/h) but in real life the speed difference between the 440 and 445 was small, although the 445 had better acceleration, particularly in the lower speed range. According to one source the 445 could accelerate in fourth gear from 22mph (35km/h) to 41mph (65km/h) in 12.5 seconds compared to 22.2 seconds for the 440.

More importantly, the more powerful Spartak could sustain some 5mph higher cruising speeds of 55-60mph (88-97km/h),

*Škoda 445 Spartak in an original 1957 advert with Prague Castle in the background. The only external difference from the 440 was horizontal bars in the upper openings of the radiator grille (as opposed to vertical bars in the 440) and the 445 badge on the bonnet.*

the same as the Octavia. Fuel economy was only marginally worse than for the smaller engine, a typical figure being around 35mpg (8l/100km). Apart from the more powerful engine, the 445 was identical to the 440 in nearly every respect. Production of the 445 started in summer 1957 and was quite slow and in all, 9375 Škoda 445s were built, which is a relatively small production run by the standards of the 1950s. The 445 was also widely exported, and about half of the 445s built were sold in Czechoslovakia, under exactly the same rules as for the 440. The price was higher at 32,850 CZK.

## ŠKODA 440 KAROSA (1956)

**THIS WAS** a sports derivative of the Spartak, designed and built in a single prototype. Škoda provided the chassis and engine while the streamlined, good-looking body was designed by Mr Otakar Diblík, a highly competent designer with a wide range of skills. It was produced by Karosa coachbuilder in the town of Vysoké Mýto, eastern Bohemia. This was the former Sodomka coachbuilder of pre-WW2 fame, now state-owned and specialising in buses and coaches.

The car was a 2+2, and a hard top could be easily fitted. Alternatively, the car could be driven with a soft top or even no roof at all! The two-tone cream-over-blue body was very light as it was made of strengthened fibreglass called Polytex and, as a result, the 440 Karosa tipped the scales at 825kg, almost 100kg less than a standard saloon. Dimensions were similar to a standard Spartak at 4070mm long and 1630mm wide, but the 440 Karosa was considerably lower at 1320mm with the hard top on.

The engine, gearbox, suspension and chassis were identical to a standard Spartak, and the standard 30-litre fuel tank was under the right rear wing, accessible from the boot. With only 40bhp on tap the Karosa was not very powerful, but thanks to much lower

*440 Karosa looked very advanced by the standards of 1956. It is one of many Czechoslovakian 'could have beens'... (Courtesy www.obrázky.cz)*

*The interior was much smarter compared to a standard Spartak. Gear change was atop the central tunnel, far more practical than column gear change. (Courtesy www.obrázky.cz)*

*This picture of the Karosa shows it displayed at a classic car show in the Czech Republic a few years ago. Sadly, it was never involved in motor sport. (Courtesy www.obrázky.cz)*

weight achieved a 75mph (120km/h) top speed. Acceleration was also described as much better than in a standard Spartak, but I have not found accurate figures. The Karosa drove well and retained the reliability of the Spartak, and fuel economy was good at 35mpg (8l/100km). We can only speculate on how it would have performed with later twin-carb Škoda engines, particularly the 1221cc, 55bhp unit fitted to the Octavia 1200 TS or Felicia Super, as described earlier.

The Karosa was revealed to the public in summer 1956 and attracted much interest. It went on to be displayed at the traditional Brno Motor and Engineering Show in the autumn of the same year, again attracting positive comments from the motoring press and public alike. Hopes for production and sales were high, but never materialised, although the reasons are unclear. One likely explanation is that the Karosa factory did not have spare capacity for production of the bodies as it had to focus on buses and coaches, and finding an alternative supplier was impossible in the directive economy.

The single prototype was in the possession of various private owners and was eventually restored to a high standard. To my understanding, it is now displayed in the Museum of Coachbuilding in Vysoké Mýto, a small town in eastern Bohemia.

## ŠKODA 440 PICK-UP

**THIS WAS** a utility version of the Spartak built as a single prototype in summer 1957. The main alterations were from the B-pillar rearwards, and instead of the rear seats and boot there was an open load area approximately 1500mm long and 1350mm wide, although the width between the rear wheelarches was only 900mm. The load

*The single prototype of the 440 Pick-up, still with overriders fitted to the bumpers. This could have been a useful light utility vehicle. Note the external rear-view mirror as fitted to Spartaks destined for export. (Courtesy www.obrázky.cz)*

area had a wooden floor and could be covered with a tarpaulin. The pick-up was mechanically identical to a standard saloon and overall dimensions were also the same except for a slightly shorter 4030mm length, the reason being the absence of overriders on both bumpers. The load capability was 200kg with a crew of two or 275kg with just a driver. Production of some 600 pick-ups was considered but never took place and I have not succeeded in finding any explanation.

## WHAT HAPPENED IN 1958?

**BY 1958** production of the Spartak was well-established, if numerically inadequate, but problems with quality described on page 26 still persisted. The workforce in Mladá Boleslav, where the Spartak was built could not be blamed as the real reason was the low quality of materials and components supplied to the factory by state-owned sub-contractors, something that caused much dissatisfaction among customers (sorry, Car Purchase Permit holders) and the Škoda workforce alike. The latter mainly consisted of highly skilled and motivated designers, engineers and workers, and many of them were working for Škoda in their second or third generation. There were also many cases of multiple members of the same family working for the company. Their dedication was unreserved and their professional pride very high. They were bitterly disappointed at being let down by the state. The whole situation is well-documented and it is fair to say that the Škoda workforce was really unhappy.

Thanks to Mr L Nachtmann, Chief Archivist at Škoda, I have been able to access the Company Annual Report for 1958. It contains numerous references to the known quality problems causing discontent (including among the employees) and suggests the ways of addressing them, albeit shrouded in some period terminology. Typically for a factory working in a Communist-controlled country, there is no reference to poor quality of materials and components delivered to Škoda by state-owned sub-contractors. There are even (strictly unofficial) stories that a strike was considered in the summer of 1958. I have looked into this quite thoroughly, but have not found sufficient evidence. However, it is likely that the regime was on a collision course with the Škoda workforce and even the Communist Party could not afford a major industrial dispute, whichever form it would have taken.

Therefore, measures were quietly taken to ensure adequate supply of good quality materials. These became widely available in early 1959, just in time for production of the Octavia. An interesting digression is that a special *StB* (State Security Police) unit was set up in late 1958; the unit was based in Mladá Boleslav and its sole task was to keep an eye on the Škoda (officially AZNP) workforce. Could it be that there *was* a real risk of a strike or protests and thereby of huge embarrassment for the regime?

## HOW DID THE SPARTAK COMPARE?

**THE SHORT** answer is 'quite well'. From 1956 onwards, the Spartak had to compete against comparable Eastern Bloc cars, but more importantly against its European counterparts. Let us deal with the Eastern Bloc competitors first as the number of small family models on offer in the 'Soviet Empire' was rather limited.

The Soviets were producing the Moskvich 402, a model in production from 1956 to 1958, so it was an almost exact contemporary of the Spartak. It was of similar size to the Spartak, but it was 130mm taller at 1560mm, which resulted in a much higher centre of gravity and inferior roadholding. It was also some 60kg heavier with a kerb weight of 980kg. The Moskvich had quite an elegant pontoon four-door saloon body, which improved access to the rear seats – important in a small family car. The four-door layout was its only advantage over the two-door Spartak. The Moskvich 402 had a four-cylinder 1220cc engine of ancient SV layout offering 35bhp. This made the car severely underpowered, and its top speed was just under 66mph (105km/h) and although I have not found acceleration figures we can safely assume that the 402 was not exactly agile. A three-speed gearbox did not help the economy either, and although figures for the 402 are not available, newer models typically returned 23-28mpg (10-12l/100km).

East Germany had the front-wheel drive Wartburg 311, production of which started in 1955. The early model was manufactured until 1961. At 4300mm the Wartburg was considerably longer than the Spartak, but its width and height were similar to its Czechoslovakian counterpart. The four-door Wartburg had by far the most elegant body of all Eastern European cars of the late 1950s, and it was also more spacious than the Spartak, but on the minus side it was very underpowered with its 900cc two-stroke three-cylinder engine. The power was a meagre 37bhp, inadequate for a car tipping the scales at 960kg. Top speed was around 66mph (105km/h) and acceleration was described as very poor, but again, I have not succeeded in finding accurate figures. The Wartburg was less economical than the Spartak, but better than the Moskvich with typical fuel economy of 25-30mpg (9.3-11.2l/100km).

Poland was manufacturing Syrena Model 100 cars, the first prototype built in December 1953 at the same time as the first Spartak. Preparations for mass production took a long time, and the first cars rolled off the production lines in March 1957. The Syrena was a two-door saloon, marginally smaller than the Spartak, although it was heavier at 950kg, possibly because it still had an ash frame. The 746cc two-stroke two-cylinder initially offered just 27bhp, which was totally inadequate, and the early Syrena was even more underpowered than the Moskvich 402 and Wartburg 311. I have found only slightly vague references to the Syrena's performance, but the top speed was probably below 62mph (100km/h). The tiny, highly stressed engine was not particularly economical and returned some 33mpg (8.5l/100km).

It is fair to say that apart from its two-door layout limiting usability (compared to the Moskvich and Wartburg) the Spartak had a clear edge over all of its Eastern European contemporaries in performance, handling and economy. Compared to the Moskvich and Syrena it was also much better built, and the build quality of the Wartburg was comparable to that of the Spartak. While the Moskvich and Wartburg were imported into Czechoslovakia, the Syrena was not.

Comparison with Western European small family cars represented a tougher challenge, even though the technical lead of the European automotive industry over the Eastern Bloc was much smaller in the 1950s than later, particularly from the 1970s onwards.

British competitors were the Morris Minor 1000 introduced in 1956 and Ford Anglia 100E. Both were technically more advanced in one important respect: they had monocoque bodies. They had the advantage of being available as two-door or four-door saloons (the Ford in Prefect guise) and the Minor, which was also available as a convertible, was slightly smaller than the Spartak. While less powerful with its 948cc 37bhp engine, it was significantly lighter at 775kg. Performance was similar to the Spartak, with top speed marginally higher and acceleration probably the same. The acceleration figures for the Spartak are hard to come by, but the limited sources available suggest a 0-62mph (0-100km/h) time of some 30-32 seconds. The fuel economy was also similar to that of the Minor. The Spartak gained some advantage with a more spacious interior and a considerably larger boot and it also featured indicator lights, the Minor's outdated trafficators not replaced until 1961.

The Anglia 100E was a smart-looking car of the modern three-box design, just like the Spartak. Compared with its Czechoslovakian counterpart, it was slightly smaller but its major weak point was the ancient SV engine dating back to the mid-1930s. The power was 36bhp from 1172cc while a three-speed gearbox was another obsolete feature. Even so, the Anglia had similar performance to the Spartak (in 440 guise), mainly on account of being much lighter (737kg vs 920kg).

It was inevitably less spacious, but more important was its poor fuel economy compared to both the Spartak and Minor; the Anglia typically returned only just over 30mpg (c9.3l/100km). Unlike in the Spartak, a heater was optional rather than standard. The Prefect 107E model had the advantage of four-door body. Comparing the Spartak with the Anglia E494A-based Popular 103E would be unfair, as this Ford was basically a pre-war design even though it remained in production as the cheapest option until 1959.

The Spartak held its own against the VW Beetle from the same period. The Beetle was similar in size, but its boot (in front) was much smaller at 140 litres although there was an additional 60 litres of storage space behind the rear seats. This was still well below the Spartak's 300-litre capacity. The Beetle was at least as well built as the Spartak and, with a kerb weight of 840kg, considerably lighter. As it was also less powerful with a 1131cc, 30bhp engine (1192cc, 34bhp from 1957), the performance of the two cars was similar and the same applied to fuel economy. Being air-cooled, the Beetle had less efficient heating compared to the Spartak.

French competitors were the Renault Dauphine, a small rear-engined saloon, and the more powerful Simca Aronde (old French for swallow, which was the logo of Simca). Both had the advantage of a four-door layout. The 845cc Dauphine was slightly smaller than the Spartak and very light at 630kg. The power output of 27bhp, later 32bhp, was therefore quite adequate.

The Dauphine was more economical than the Spartak, typically returning around 40mpg (7l/100km) while achieving a similar top speed but slower acceleration. Despite problems with the quality of some components, build quality and reliability gave the Spartak an edge. The Aronde had either a 1090cc engine with 40bhp or 1290cc giving 48bhp and was more comfortable with a better ride. The 1290cc model was also faster than the Spartak (even the 445 model) and could accelerate better.

The most powerful, relatively rare Aronde-Elysée model (not to be confused with the P60 Elysée, see chapter 13) was tested by *The Motor* magazine in late 1956. Top speed was recorded as 82.6mph (132.9km/h), acceleration was 23.9 seconds from 0 to 60mph (97km/h). The Spartak could not match such performance, although standard Octavias came close and, in TS and 1200 TS form, exceeded it considerably, particularly in terms of acceleration. It should also be said that many lower-powered Arondes were only marginally faster than the Spartak. Fuel economy of the Aronde was slightly worse at some 33mpg (c8.5l/100km) being typical. On balance, the Aronde was still a better car overall.

In summary, the Spartak could hold its own against the majority of comparable European cars, having some advantages and some disadvantages. It was also reasonably priced in export markets, but unlike Škodas of the 1970s and 1980s the Spartak was not the cheapest car on the market; it was rather middle-of-the-range. Given the combination of decent quality and sensible prices the export success of the Spartak is no surprise. A good service network in Europe and a supply of spare parts (often at the expense of the domestic market) were other advantages.

The Spartak is quite a popular classic in my old country today, although much rarer than the Octavia. Spare parts supply is good with substantial secondary production, and Spartak owners also benefit from the fact that some parts are interchangeable with the Octavia.

## THE INTERMEDIATE MODEL

**THE INTERMEDIATE** Model (Mezityp in Czech) was a hybrid of Spartak chassis with transverse leaf springs front and rear and more modern Octavia body, and it went into production in early January 1959. Initially, they were built in parallel with Spartaks, but these were phased out by late-January 1959. The Intermediate Model remained in production until mid-March 1959 and 3200 were built, but very few have survived in my old country and they are now sought after because of their rarity.

## ŠKODA 450 TYPE 984 (1957-1959)

**THE IDEA** of a sports car based on the Spartak started taking shape in 1956. One of the results was the great-looking Karosa which, unfortunately, did not go into production. Unlike the Karosa, the Škoda 450 was a completely in-house effort. Interestingly, the initial inspiration came from the 1955 Earls Court Motor Show, a group of designers from Škoda was allowed to travel to the UK to visit the show. They were impressed by British sports cars such as the MG TF and, above all, the brand new MGA, and a decision was made to try and design a Škoda sports car that would be destined mainly for export markets, particularly Western Europe. Higher echelons of the Communist Party generally disliked sports cars, perceiving them as 'bourgeois' or 'decadent', but the regime was desperate for hard currency and practical considerations prevailed on this occasion.

Inevitably, the car had to be based on the Spartak, as no alternative was available. The actual development started in the Kvasiny plant in early-1956 and the prototype was built by the spring. The chassis from a Spartak could be used, but the car needed a lighter, sportier body and a more powerful engine. The reliable OHV 1089cc straight-four was modified for a higher compression ratio of 8.4:1 as opposed to 6.8:1 in the Spartak, the camshaft was altered and the engine was now higher-revving at 5500rpm when giving maximum power. Two Czechoslovakian-made Jikov (pronounced *Ee-kov*) carburettors, slightly modified compared to the standard single Spartak item, were fitted, and the engine offered 50bhp and torque of 75Nm.

The prototype had a convertible body that was completely different to the Spartak from the bulkhead rearwards, and the windscreen was also different, almost panoramic. The new Škoda was a 2+2 roadster with a fabric roof, and was marginally lighter than the Spartak, tipping the scales at 900kg. Interestingly, the boot capacity was similar to that of the Spartak, approaching 300 litres, even though the boot was shallower. Top speed was around 82mph (130km/h) and acceleration was much quicker compared to the Spartak. Unfortunately, accurate figures are scarce, but I have found that the 450 could sprint

*450 was indeed similar in appearance to the early model Felicia, but technical differences were substantial as will be described.*

from 0 to 50mph (80km/h) in 14 seconds and fuel consumption was slightly higher, typically just over 31mpg (9l/100km). The prototype still had a column gear change, but the dashboard was smarter than that of the Spartak, and all 450s had a clock fitted in the centre. There was a front bench seat and two small seats in the rear, only suitable for children, or adults on (very) short trips.

A considerable amount of road testing was done by the autumn of 1956, and the new Škoda would be exhibited at the traditional Motor and Engineering Show in Brno, Moravia. This took place in October 1956 and the Škoda Sport, as the car was now referred to, attracted much interest. Further development continued afterwards with the shape of the boot area and boot lid changed and the rear of the car made lower. That improved its appearance significantly. Two more prototypes followed in 1957 and the name was changed to Škoda 450 denoting four cylinders and 50bhp. A new radiator grille similar to the later Felicia was introduced at an early stage of development, the decorative 'propeller' typical of Spartaks and early Octavias was deleted and the grille consisted of horizontal and vertical bars.

Ten Škoda 450s were built in 1957 for further road testing; they performed well and their reliability was good. One was displayed at the Brno Motor and Engineering Show in September 1957, another at the Earls Court Motor Show in London the following month. The Škoda company had contacted current Miss USA, Charlotte Sheffield, who was in London at the time and she agreed to pose for photographers in front of the 450 displayed at the show. This probably increased interest in the new sporty Škoda, but the production could not keep up ...

Production started in the 'shadow' Kvasiny factory in June 1958. Production cars were identical to the final prototypes, including the column gear change, and all 450s had a fabric roof; a hard top only became available for the Felicia. Production was slow and early cars had problems with

*The dashboard and seats of the 450 were much more elegant compared to the Spartak, but the column gear change was not very practical in a sports car. The steering was identical to the Spartak's.*

insufficient torsional strength of the body; the scuttle-shake common in convertibles was quite pronounced in the 450 but the problem was resolved by fitting additional strengthening struts, particularly to the sills. The 450 was offered on the newly introduced so-called 'free market', without the need for obtaining the Car Purchase Permit.

However, the price was 42,000 CZK, an equivalent of at least 30 average monthly salaries. Only 300 Škoda 450s were sold in Czechoslovakia, with 700 exported to various Western European countries, and unlike Felicias they were not exported to Eastern European countries. Production ended in February 1959 with a total of 1010 cars built including the batch of 10 for road-testing in 1957. One 450 is exhibited in the Škoda Museum in Mladá Boleslav but they are extremely rare in my old country and to see one at a classic car show you have to be very lucky. They are often mistaken for the outwardly similar, much more common Felicias.

## CHAPTER 3

# MY MEMORIES OF THE OCTAVIA

**NOW, I** must be honest: I love the Octavia (Oktávka in colloquial Czech) and will have difficulty in avoiding bias. My parents' first car was an early model Octavia. They bought it in 1960 when I was aged three and I loved that green car from the word go. When I was well-behaved, I was allowed to sit in the front passenger seat with two big cushions under my bottom so I could see out. Well, safety awareness was almost non-existent in 1960! A little later, I was promoted to be my dad's co-pilot and asked to switch on the wipers or headlights as required. We played that lovely game where my dad would ask me in a formal voice like via an intercom: "Captain to the co-pilot. Mirek, switch on the headlights, please!" I replied as a proper co-pilot should: "Yes Sir, I'm switching on the headlights now!" ... and thrived on the responsibility.

My parents had gone through the whole Car Purchase Permit nonsense, although the rules were slightly relaxed by 1960. They must have been: the Permit was given to my mum who was a junior doctor at the time. The regime decided to pretend it had a caring attitude and make health professionals 'deserving applicants'. Just a small digression: the Czechoslovakian health care system was tax-funded, free for patients and of good quality. In fact, it was in many ways modelled on the British NHS, a fact of life that the Communists would vigorously deny.

Going back to the Octavia, my mum was even allowed to choose a colour! Just how my parents achieved that I do not know. Bribing someone in the Mototechna dealership was one option, but like most Czechoslovakians at the time my parents resented bribery and tried to avoid it if at all possible. Or maybe someone wanted to please my mum, then a good-looking young lady ... whose looks I have not inherited. The story in our family goes that mum chose bright green to go well with her new dress. I am quite prepared to believe it given all the recollections I have of my mum.

The green Octavia stayed with our family for five years and, as far as I recall, never let us down. My parents drove it to France in summer 1961 (and I helped as my dad's co-pilot!) when my dad, a fluent French speaker, was offered a job representing his employer (a state-owned commercial company) in Paris. The Octavia took us for many long trips, including to France's Atlantic coast, and proved highly reliable. We returned to Prague in late 1964. I really missed the Octavia after my parents upgraded to a modern Ford Cortina Mk 1 in 1965. Realistically, the Cortina was a better car (so it should be as it was one generation more modern!), but I did not see it that way as an eight-year -old. It took me some time to grow fond of the Cortina.

My dad was the main driver in the family as my mum was not that keen on driving. He loved the Octavia and considered it far superior to other new cars available in Czechoslovakia in 1960: the weedy two-stroke Wartburg 311 from East Germany and the thirsty, cumbersome Soviet Moskvich 407. With my current knowledge, I have no doubt that my dad was right ... and that is my impartial view!

*Octavia for Ukraine, May 2022. My son-in-law's dad and I took the Octavia from Warsash, Hampshire to Edinburgh and back (900+ mile round trip) for a fundraising drive to support the British Red Cross Ukraine Appeal. Here we are crossing the Scottish border. We raised a significant sum of money and the Old Girl performed faultlessly.*

*Prestatyn Classic Car Show, August 2024. My brother-in-law and I drove from Warsash to Prestatyn, North Wales (270+ miles), supported by our family and friends. We were fundraising for the Trekstock charity, supporting young adults with cancer, lymphoma and leukaemia. Again, we raised a considerable sum. The Old Girl was declared the Car of the Show and was also the winner of the 1945-1960 class.*

One other small family car available was the French Simca Aronde. This was imported in limited numbers, more expensive and offered (via the Car Purchase Permit system) mainly to fairly distinguished but not top-ranking Comrades. Yes, I am serious, the distinguished Comrades were rewarded by being offered a 'posh' Western European car! While not remotely posh, the Octavia could hold its own very well against the Aronde, but not so well against the updated Simca Elysée P60.

CHAPTER 4

# OCTAVIA PROTOTYPES

**FIRST STUDIES** for a future successor to the Spartak started in late 1956, when production of the car was gaining pace. It was recognised that while the Spartak was performing well, it was not a groundbreaking design and would be at a major disadvantage against modern European cars within two to three years. Development was focussed on improving the ride and handling by alterations to the chassis and suspension, the best way forward being to replace the transverse leaf springs front and rear with coil springs. Building of prototypes thus equipped started in early 1957 and by the summer six prototypes were completed. These were designated Š 440P and extensively tested, and significant improvements were noticed in terms of both ride and handling.

Unfortunately, a major problem soon

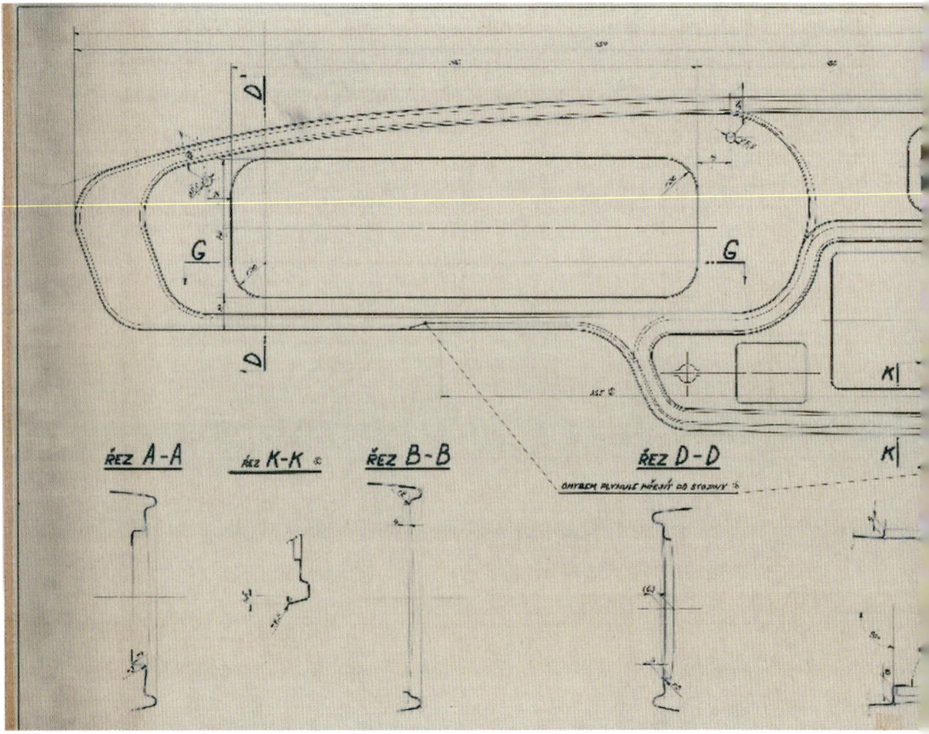

arose: the rear coil springs required telescopic shock absorbers of good quality to obtain the full advantage of this layout. The (only available, state-owned) external sub-contractor supplying the shock absorbers was struggling to deliver sufficient numbers, but struggled even more with quality issues. It could not be realistically assumed that the issues would be resolved in the foreseeable future. The limitations of the directive economy manifested themselves yet again. The sub-contractor knew full well that there was no competition, so its managing director focussed on fulfilling the delivery quotas as required by the State Plan. The quotas had high priority and the quality was secondary; in view of this, the decision was made to fit coil springs only in front, while a transverse leaf spring at the rear was retained. It was,

*Above: This small picture shows the Š 440P prototype chassis as it was in late 1957 with the traditional central tube but coil springs front and rear. (Courtesy www.autorevue.cz)*

*Below: Drawing of the early Octavia Type 985/993 dashboard, interestingly, for a right-hand-drive car! (Courtesy Škoda archive, Mladá Boleslav, Czech Republic)*

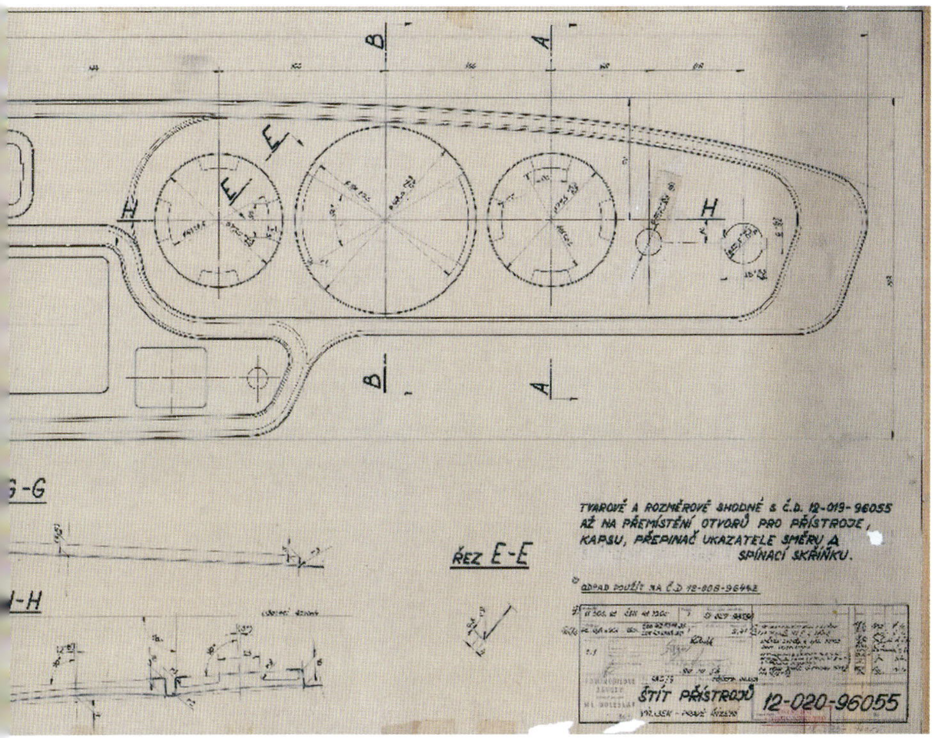

*One of the Octavia prototypes on an original promotional picture probably from late 1958. The car has non-standard two-tone paint. (Courtesy Škoda archive, Mladá Boleslav, Czech Republic)*

however, made stronger as well as more compliant by increasing the number of leaves, which were also slightly thinner than before. This compromise solution retained much of the improved ride and handling.

The later prototypes had more differences from the Spartak, one of them the new dashboard without the elevated cluster of three dials typical of the Spartak. The speedometer calibrated to 140km/h (88mph) with odometer was flanked by the slightly smaller diameter fuel gauge on the left and coolant temperature indicator on the right. The figures on Spartak dials were black against the white background, which now became the other way round, and the dials were placed in the more elegant straight dashboard. This layout also made them easier to see, while the glovebox on the front passenger's side was now open. This dashboard was fitted to the early production Octavias Type 985 and 993 built until January 1961.

The radiator grille had just one opening like the production Octavias, while the decorative 'propeller' was retained, and there was the traditional Škoda logo, with the winged arrow on the 'propeller' hub. In my view, the 'propeller' is a nice feature of early Octavias and makes them look very smart. The only difference was that the Škoda inscription was on the front panel rather than the bonnet, as on production Octavias.

One of the prototypes was shown to the public at the 'May Day Rally of The Working People' in Mladá Boleslav on 1 May 1958. Such events took place all over the country and it was advisable to attend. The Š 440P attracted much attention, and another prototype was exhibited at the elegance contest in Wiesbaden, then West Germany, in summer 1958 and awarded a Golden Ribbon. This car had smart two-tone paint, although unfortunately that was not offered on production Octavias.

As the prototypes performed well, it was planned to start production of the Octavia in late-summer 1958. However, the factory was still experiencing problems with the quality of various materials and components (see Chapter 2). Production of the new model was therefore postponed until early 1959, but on the plus side, the Octavia then benefitted from much better materials which contributed to its renowned build quality.

CHAPTER 5

# OCTAVIA TYPE 985 AND OCTAVIA SUPER TYPE 993 (1959-1960)

**FULL PRODUCTION** of the Octavia and Octavia Super started simultaneously in early March 1959. Prior to that, some Octavias were built from January 1959 onwards, but the majority of production was the Intermediate Model (see Chapter 2). The number of Octavias built in January and February 1959 is unclear, one source indicates 412 cars.

The new model was outwardly similar to the Spartak, but technically quite different. However, the traditional layout with the engine in front and the rear-wheel drive was retained. Most of the alterations had been tested on the prototypes. The front axle was completely new, with the transverse leaf spring replaced by coil springs, which significantly improved ride and handling. The transverse semi-elliptical leaf spring in the rear had now more leaves, which further improved ride comfort. The tubular chassis remained the same as in the Spartak, but the wheelbase was marginally reduced from 2400mm to 2390mm.

One invisible change was the fitting of softer, better quality engine and body mounts. This further improved ride. Initially, the same engines were fitted as to the Spartak. The engines were slightly uprated in the autumn of 1960 by increasing the compression ratio to 7.5. This increased power of the 1089cc engine to 42bhp. The larger engine now offered 47bhp. Both uprated engines were slightly higher-revving, giving the maximum output at 4500rpm. They were initially not fitted consistently, but became standard in early 1961 when the Octavia was modernised.

The gearbox had four speeds with synchromesh on all gears but first, as in late production Spartaks. A column gear change was retained and a larger clutch made gear changes slicker, which improved acceleration. Screw-and-nut steering remained unchanged. Hydraulic drum brakes were now more effective, with improved, larger brake shoes and a longer, lower diameter brake master cylinder. The new master cylinder reduced the force required by the pedal for effective braking. The use of good quality materials also made a difference. The early Octavia had the same 30-litre fuel tank under the passenger-side rear wing as the Spartak. The lockable filler cap was atop the wing.

The completely new impact-absorbing steering column significantly improved safety. The ivory-colour steering wheel was new with an additional inner ring. This could be gently pulled by one finger of each hand to operate the horn. The improvement of ergonomics was quite major. Previously, a Spartak driver had to take one hand off the steering wheel and push the button on its hub. New dashboard similar to that of the later Š 440P prototypes was introduced. One other change was that the background of the dials was now black and the figures white. This made reading easier compared to the Spartak dials with white background and black figures. The new layout was generally more elegant and easier to follow. There were three knobs on the dashboard: the choke was just right of the steering column and had a blue centre, while the starter was further to the right and had a red centre.

To start the engine the driver needed to turn the ignition key to the right (the ignition barrel was just left of the steering column) and then pull the starter knob. Use of the choke (this too was of pull-out type) was recommended when the ambient temperature was low. Another pull-out knob was for the headlights. There were also toggle switches operating the wipers, heater, internal lighting and optional foglights. The early Octavias had front bench seats, but now with separate adjustable backrests. The Octavia also introduced the optional conversion of seats into simple beds. The front bench could be moved forward on its rails, and the separate backrests could be completely reclined. This moderately comfortable arrangement could sleep two adults and up to two children. My parents' Octavia had this option and it came in handy on several occasions! Somewhat disappointingly, my light blue Octavia does not have it. A heater was standard on all Octavias.

External appearance also changed: the decorative 'propeller' in front of the radiator grille was retained, but the shape of the grille was simplified, now with perpendicular, slightly concave bars. There was now just one opening instead of the original three as tested on the prototypes. The tail lights were more effective, if still of the same size. The front bumper was now divided into two parts, and the registration plate was placed in a hinged frame directly fitted to the front valance. The frame with plate could be unclipped to gain access to the opening into which a starting handle could be inserted. Like Spartaks, all early (and updated) Octavias were two-door saloons. Unfortunately, the four-door option was never offered.

While it represented a major improvement on the Spartak, the Octavia was not a cutting edge design. It retained a separate chassis, although the all-independent suspension with coil springs in front was an advanced feature in 1959. The Octavia was an honest car built to a high standard, with good quality materials now available (see Chapter 2). This resulted in excellent reliability and longevity. Properly maintained Octavias could cover 125,000 to 155,000 miles (200,000 to 250,000 kilometres) before the engine needed major attention.

The gearbox, steering and suspension were also tough, and the body resisted rust well. Even in quite old Octavias, corrosion usually was not a major problem, partly because the often affected sills were not structural.

The Octavia had some seemingly minor features showing how well-designed it was. The bonnet was statically balanced, therefore it stayed open in any chosen position and no strut was required. The spacious engine bay offered good access to all important components, but also had shallow recesses for putting tools (or a cup of tea) safely! The main technical details for both the Octavia and Octavia Super are given in Table 6.

The relatively high ground clearance of 175mm came in handy on very rough surfaces. The Octavia was a compact car, marginally lighter than the Spartak, with a typical kerb weight around 900kg. Top speed was stated as being the same as the Spartak, but the official figures were an underestimate; in real life Octavias were certainly faster and livelier than their Spartak predecessors. They typically achieved 72-75mph (115-120km/h) with little difference between the Octavia and Octavia Super.

Well-sorted Octavias of both models could only just top 75mph (120km/h), but this would have stressed the engine excessively and, if done frequently, would have shortened its useful life. Fuel economy would have also suffered significantly. Stories about Octavias doing 78mph (125km/h) should be taken with a pinch of salt, and I even saw a self-declared Octavia owner claiming in an online discussion that he could achieve 82mph (130km/h) with his standard Octavia, not a TS (see Chapter 9). In my view, this is pure fantasy.

Both models could cruise at 55-60mph (88-97km/h) for any length of time, and in

TABLE 6

| Škoda Octavia Type 985/Octavia Super Type 993 (1959-1960) | |
|---|---|
| Length | 4065mm |
| Width | 1600mm |
| Height | 1430mm |
| Wheelbase | 2390mm |
| Kerb weight | 900kg/910kg |
| Bore x stroke | 68x75mm/72x75mm |
| Capacity | 1089cc/1221cc |
| Power | 40bhp/45bhp at 4200rpm* |
| Compression ratio | 7.0:1 |
| Top speed | 69mph (110km/h)/ 72mph (115km/h)** |
| Acceleration | 0-62mph (0-100km/h) 28/26 seconds |
| Average economy | 37mpg (7.6l/100km)/35mpg (8l/100km) |

**These figures relate to the earlier engines*
***In reality Octavias were quicker – see text.*

my experience, the Octavia is quite happy sitting on the motorway within that speed range all day long, with some reserve of power if required. The Octavia Super had slightly more grunt and accelerated better, but again the difference was barely noticeable (personal communication from Octavia owners and my own experience). Figures for acceleration are quite hard to obtain, although I have found a number of figures for the 0-62mph (0-100km/h) time, varying quite widely from 25 to 35 seconds. The former is somewhat optimistic, the latter grossly underestimates the Octavia's abilities. Most sources give figures of about 28 seconds, which sounds realistic to me. I had even more difficulties finding the figures for the Octavia Super, but it could probably do the 'sprint' in about 26 seconds.

Fuel economy was good, with the smaller engine marginally better. Overall, the differences between the two models were minimal, although we can speculate that it might have been more appropriate to separate the Octavias more, such as fitting a 1.3- or 1.4-litre engine to the Octavia Super.

All Octavias had very good roadholding, including in wet or icy conditions. They were originally fitted with crossply tyres in a size of 5.50x15, later 5.90x15 and although Octavias for export to Western Europe probably had radial tyres from about 1960, available sources are not entirely clear. It is therefore perfectly appropriate (and safer) to run a classic Octavia on radial tyres. My Octavia has 165/15 R80 radials, so slightly wider than the original crossplies, and this is an excellent choice, striking the right balance between roadholding and agility.

In contrast to their somewhat sedate appearance, Octavias were surprisingly manoeuvrable, with neutral handling and a decent turning circle. That stood them in good stead in rallies, often against quicker opponents, and the reason was the all-independent suspension and superb weight distribution between the front and rear axles approaching 50:50 (48:52 to be precise). It is a matter of regret that the Octavia was not yet fitted with rack-and-pinion steering, which would have improved handling further still.

Another advantage of the Octavia (shared with the Spartak) was its highly efficient cooling system, with the capacity of 6.9 litres. This made overheating very unlikely as long as the radiator, thermostat and cooling jacket of the engine were in good condition. In fact, I had a personal experience with this: the original radiator of my Octavia was silted up and its capacity reduced to some 4.5 litres, and as a result, the engine had a tendency to overheat even though the cooling jacket was not affected. Once the radiator was replaced, the problem disappeared. When we got stuck in extremely heavy traffic in Prague, the coolant temperature rose slowly from 80 to 85 degrees centigrade and no further.

I can confirm both the performance and economy figures from my own experience. When Frank Anderson and I drove the light blue Octavia from Prague to the UK, we both achieved 70mph (112km/h) on occasions and the Octavia still accelerated quite well. We probably could have achieved 75mph (120km/h) on a German *Autobahn*, but that would have been rather irresponsible. Typical fuel economy of my car is some 36mpg (7.8l/100km) in mixed driving, and very representative of this model.

Prices in 1959 were 28,500 CZK for the Octavia and 38,500 CZK for the Octavia Super. This was an equivalent of 22 and nearly 30 average monthly salaries respectively. The Super was sold on the so-called free market with no Car Purchase Permit required, which was supposed to justify the high price.

The interior offered sufficient space to carry four people in comfort (by the standards of the time!) and five over short distances. In fact, the Octavia feels fairly comfortable even today, helped by the good balance between the ride and handling, and the boot offered a decent capacity of 300 litres with a spare wheel in a cradle made of steel tubing.

The Octavia was available in more colours than the Spartak, which could be purchased in about five colours (I have not succeeded in finding details of Spartak colours). Some lucky Car Purchase Permit holders (including my mum) could now even choose their colours! The shades offered in spring 1959 included ivory, light yellow, light grey, light blue, dark blue, bright green, turquoise, medium brown, burgundy and black. White was added in 1960, but very few Octavias were delivered in that colour.

*My 1960 Octavia shortly after I bought it, just outside Prague in July 2014. The decorative chrome sideskirts are missing at this point. It is a 1089cc model, exactly the same as my parents' first car except it does not have the bed conversion option. The Octavia had been laid up in a shed for a number of years, neither driven nor maintained, before being 'commercially restored'. The 'quality' of restoration was a good negotiating point when discussing the price! Proper restoration then took place in the UK.*

VZORNÍK BAREV KAROSÉRIÍ ŠKODA OCTAVIA, OCTAVIA COMBI a FELICIA.

| Octavia 1959-1960 | Octavia 1961-1964 | Octavia Combi 1961-1971 | Felicia 1959-1960 | Felicia 1961-1964 |
|---|---|---|---|---|
| 1959-60 16 | 1961-62 16 | 1961-62 16 | 1959-60 16 | 1961-64 58 |
| 1959-60 11 | 1961 060 | 1961-64 407 | 1959-60 11 | 1961-62 060 |
| 1959-60 18 | 1961-64 076 | 1961-71 9 | 1959-60 18 | 1961-62 39 |
| 1959-60 9 | 1961-64 9 | 1963-64 510 | 1959-60 403 | 1961-64 407 |
| 1959-60 37 | 1961-64 407 | 1963-64 401 | 1959-60 031 | 1961-64 9 |
| 1959-60 67 | 1961 10 | 1964-67 605 | 1959-60 9 | 1961-64 031 |
| 1959-60 39 | 1961 031 | 1964-67 515 | 1959-60 10 | 1963-64 803 |
| 1959-60 41 | 1963-64 111 | 1965-70 031 | 1959-60 39 | 1963-64 602 |
| 1959-60 10 | 1963-64 510 | 1968-71 413 | 1959-60 39 | 1964 605 |
| | 1963-64 401 | 1968-71 | | |
| | 1963-64 58 | 1968-71 | | |
| | 1964 515 | 1968-71 | | |
| | 1964 605 | 1963-71 58 | | |

* Vozy byly lakovány syntetickým vypalovacím emailem Autex S-2016, vypalovaným při teplotě 130 - 135°C.

* Tento barevník je pouze orientační, neboť tón jednotlivých odstínů barev v něm vyobrazených, může být poněkud odlišný od skutečného.

*This poor-quality copy (the only one I could find) shows the list of colour options available for Octavias and Felicias, covering the whole production run. My light blue 1960 Octavia is No 18 in the first column on the left. While the offer is seemingly wide, not all colours were available at the same time.*

*This early example is of the same colour as my parents' Octavia. The external rear-view mirror on the driver side front wing is non-standard. Early Octavias had just internal rear-view mirrors. Many cars had external mirrors retrofitted (to the wings or doors) when they became available as an after-market accessory from about 1962.*

The interiors were of relatively light colours, but easy to keep clean. All early Octavias had seats with a combination of good quality cloth and imitation leather, the latter also used for the door cards while the rubber floormats emphasised the purposeful character of the Octavia. All materials were of considerably better quality compared to the Spartak. In keeping with the standards of the late 1950s, there was an ashtray in the middle of the dashboard and another two on each side for the rear passengers.

Early Octavias were not equipped with radios; in fact there was no space in the dashboard for fitting one. Even so, a few Octavias had a radio inserted at the lower edge of the dashboard in a rather makeshift manner. Some early Octavias had fog lights fitted to the front bumper, but the vast majority did not have them. My Octavia originally had them, but they were not working well and I have removed them.

Total production of the early model was 56,252 Octavias and 24,057 Octavia Supers, this representing less than one quarter of all Octavias built, and less than one third of Supers. The early models are therefore considerably rarer than the updated model from 1961 onwards, and are sought after, although most enthusiasts do not mind which model they buy. In particular, the choice between an Octavia and a Super is of little importance. As with many classics, they should be bought on condition rather than specification. Mechanical problems can, in general, be sorted more easily than rotten bodywork. However, as the Octavia has a separate chassis, even body corrosion is mostly repairable, although one terminal, if rare problem, is a seriously rotten chassis, where replacement is the only answer.

As my parents had an early Octavia, I much preferred one to the later (and in some respects technically better) 1961-on model. Finding my 1960 Octavia was neither quick nor easy, but the result was worth the effort!

*This picture shows the dashboard of an early Octavia (compare with the Spartak cabin in chapter 2). The light colours are typical of the Octavia. Note the sunvisors for both the driver and front passenger, fitted as standard. The small storage space on the right is now open. This Octavia has been heavily modified: it has a floor gear change and a radio. (Courtesy Zdeněk Patera, www.auta5p.eu)*

*This New Forest pony seems to like my now properly restored 1960 Octavia.*

CHAPTER 6

# OCTAVIA AS A TOWING CAR

**YES, IT** did happen. When Czechoslovakian car production was gathering pace around 1960, and car ownership started increasing significantly, some car owners became interested in caravanning. However, their options were limited. The most modern and powerful car available to 'The Working People' was the Octavia, and while there were some Tatra T603s and Volga M21s, these were mainly used by the Communist Party, *StB* secret police and state-owned companies. Very few were available to private owners. The caravan had to be very small and light, so that it could be towed by an Octavia (or possibly a Moskvich). There were still substantial numbers of pre-war cars on the road, but most of them were not sufficiently powerful for towing. As for the 900cc Wartburg, it was hard pressed to move under its own steam ... call me rude and biased!

The designer and producer was the Karosa company, state-owned from 1948 (previously the famous Sodomka coachbuilders), which was mainly building buses and coaches, although it had some previous experience in designing and building caravans. Sodomka coachbuilder had designed and built W1 (larger) and W2 (smaller) caravans in the late 1930s. Both models went into production, but this was limited to a total of 59 caravans, about 40 of them W1s.

The company was ordered by the German occupiers to resume production in 1942; the new military model was designated W3 and used as a mobile laboratory, radio cabin or command centre by the German Army. Production was slow (Czech employees were not tremendously efficient when they had to work for the Nazis) and gave a total of 70 W3s. With their decent level of expertise and experience the Karosa team designed a very good-looking small caravan able to accommodate two adults and two children.

The team brought in an external designer, Mr Otakar Diblík, who was already highly successful at the time, and he completed the design in late 1959. Diblík designed a highly elegant, quite aerodynamic body made of polyester glass fibre, which eliminated the risk of corrosion and reduced weight. The 3700mm long, fully equipped caravan tipped the scales at 400kg. This was very good, and the W4 Dingo could be towed by an Octavia, although the 1221cc Super with higher torque was considered more suitable for towing than the standard 1089cc Octavia. The name Dingo did attract my interest, but I have not succeeded in finding how it had come about.

The Dingo was quite comfortable by the standards of 1960. There was a small table and benches that could be easily converted into simple beds, and a small foldable kitchen work top was available, with sufficient space for a small gas cooker. The whole design was light and airy, helped by a large skylight in the roof. Overall, the Dingo was well-designed, well-made and suitable for its purpose.

It was launched in spring 1960 and also

*Early Octavia with a W4 Dingo caravan in tow. The caravan was comparable to European products of the period. The Octavia has decorative wheelcaps, an after-market feature. The two-tone paint with probably white roof is definitely non-standard, although a few Octavias were given two-tone paint by specialist car paintshops. The number of Octavias customised in this way probably remained in single or low double figures.*

exhibited at the Czechoslovakian Exhibition taking place at the same time in the Ukrainian capital Kyiv, then the Soviet Union. Unfortunately, sales did not take off, the main reason being the price of 20,000 CZK, an equivalent of 15 average monthly salaries. In addition to the price of an Octavia, this was unaffordable for the vast majority of Czechoslovakians. Another reason was that opportunities for camping and caravanning abroad were very limited and international travel was rather restricted even within the Eastern Bloc, ie between supposedly allied nations(!). Production took place in the Karosa factory in the town of Hořice, north-eastern Bohemia, but it ceased in 1961. Total production was only 47 Dingos. The few survivors are now very sought after in my old country. In the unlikely event they come up for sale, they are absurdly expensive.

## CHAPTER 7

# OCTAVIA GOES EAST

**IT WAS** not uncommon in pre-war Czechoslovakia for explorers and car enthusiasts to set off for long drives across Europe, or even further afield. One such adventurer and writer was František Alexander Elstner (1902-1974) who became famous for several long drives with small two-stroke Aero 662 and larger but still two-stroke Aero 30 cars in 1933 and 1934 respectively. Although the Aeros were completely reliable, he then changed over to a more substantial Škoda Popular 1100 OHV Type 927 (see Chapter 2) for his exploration of the USA and Latin America.

Elstner described his experiences in several books, which became popular mainly with young people. WW2 and Nazi occupation put a stop to his activities, but he resumed them after the Liberation. This time he toured Africa with his wife and son, driving a small two-stroke Aero Minor car, and they returned to Czechoslovakia in December 1947. This trip is described in more detail in my other book *Cars from my Old Country*. His exploring was stopped once again by the Communist take-over in February 1948. He was seen as 'non-standard and potentially problematic', not the best recommendation in the eyes of Communist officials, and he ended up working as a labourer in the construction industry, but thankfully not in a labour camp.

The regime did relax by the late 1950s – in fact the difference from the early 1950s was quite noticeable. The social climate was much less oppressive, people were able to engage spontaneously in various activities without risking their liberty or even life. Elstner realised that there might be opportunities for further exploring, more so because he was allowed to publish once again, so he asked the authorities for permission to make another trip, this time to the Soviet Union. The USSR was the only viable option for a would-be explorer in 1959. Western Europe was still out of the question, the US or Canada even more so.

Even going to Africa would have been frowned upon by some Communist officials. However, it was difficult to deny permission to travel to the Soviet Union. The application was granted and Elstner could take the next step: finding a suitable car. He approached the Škoda company (well, *AZNP*) and asked whether it would be able to lend him a Spartak or even Octavia. The response from Škoda was very positive as it still remembered his pre-war trips, and Elstner shared his planned route to Moscow (via Warsaw, Minsk and Smolensk) and then further south to the Crimea before turning back west. The Škoda management offered him a brand-new Octavia with a 1089cc engine and which was customised with two-tone paint, in a smart combination of red and white. To my knowledge, this was the only Octavia in such a paint scheme.

Elstner and his friend Mr Jan Fiala set off from the Škoda factory in Mladá Boleslav on 1 August 1959. They headed north-east to the town of Hradec Králové and further to Český Těšín on the Polish border. The next stop was Warsaw, after which they headed east and crossed the Polish-Soviet border in Brest, and from there the Octavia headed to Minsk (now the capital of Belarus), coping admirably with Soviet roads ... and non-roads! That is no exaggeration as many smaller roads (an equivalent of B-roads and even some A-roads) were still just gravel tracks in 1959.

The trip continued via Smolensk to Moscow, where the explorers stayed for a few days, and then from Moscow the route took the explorers down south to the Crimea. They visited Yalta and met (probably by coincidence) a new Tchaika (*Russian for Seagull*) GAZ-13 prototype, a large six-cylinder car for high-ranking Soviet officials, but those not sufficiently high-ranking to deserve a ZIL. There was also a Volga M21 and a Pobeda (*Russian for Victory*) M20 as support vehicles. Both Czech explorers had a friendly conversation with the Soviet test drivers before carrying on. They embarked on a ship to Sochi and from there continued into the Caucasus and Georgia. The home-bound route took them via the Crimea, southern Ukraine, Kyiv, Moldavia and Romania, and from Bucharest they headed north-west into Hungary and via Budapest to Bratislava, the capital of Slovakia. They returned to Prague on 29 September 1959. The Octavia covered just over 8800 miles (14,000km) with no problems, further enhancing the model's already emerging reputation for excellent reliability.

CHAPTER 8

# OCTAVIA TYPE 702 AND OCTAVIA SUPER TYPE 703 (1961-1964)

**PRODUCTION OF** the upgraded Octavia began in early January 1961, the new model technically almost identical to its predecessor, with 1089cc, 42bhp and 1221cc, 47bhp engines now standard. The compression ratio increased to 7.5:1, which required petrol of at least 70 octane grade, which was readily available in Czechoslovakia and all existing or potential export markets by then. The mechanical starter motor was replaced by an electrical item in left-hand drive cars. Right-hand drive cars retained a mechanical starter, because the electrical item was larger and its installation would have required major alterations to the connecting rods of the gear selector as well as the hydraulic brake system.

The gearbox, steering and brakes were the same as on the earlier Octavia, although the gear selection was now slightly different, with first gear selected by pushing the lever away and up, while second gear was selected by pushing the lever away and down. In the early Octavia, third and fourth gear were selected in this manner, while first and second were closer to the driver. The handbrake remained of the umbrella handle type, placed left of the steering column, and the steering wheel was carried over.

The dimensions of the new model were identical to its predecessor. Not every new car had to be bigger than the earlier model in those days! The wheelbase remained unchanged at 2390mm, and kerb weight also remained the same at around 900kg.

Performance and fuel economy were largely unchanged, although the factory gave a top speed for the modernised Octavia of 72mph (115km/h). For the Super the official figure was now 74mph (118km/h). Acceleration figures are hard to find, but they are probably the same as for the early model, and I very much doubt that any noticeable difference could be found between the early and updated Octavia in terms of performance and economy. Good roadholding, handling and ride were retained, and the updated Octavia was also just as well built, as tough and reliable as the earlier model.

The obvious differences were external. A new radiator grille without the decorative 'propeller' was introduced, and the rear wings now had small fins with larger brake and direction indicator lights, which made the Octavia look more in keeping with the early 1960s than late 1950s. The chrome bumpers with overriders were the same as on the early Octavia, and a new handle on the boot lid was introduced in 1962 – this was shorter and wider. The access to the fuel tank was now covered by a small flap flush with the passenger-side rear wing, and the flap could only be opened by a cable from the inside. The cable was operated by a small ring placed close to the B-pillar. The fuel tank still had a 30-litre capacity, which gave a safe range of only just over 200 miles (320km), the same as the early model.

The interior was more sophisticated and the starting procedure was simplified by introducing a three-position ignition barrel: 0 for ignition off, 1 for ignition on and 2 for

*Cabin of an updated Octavia. The upper part of the dashboard is covered in soft black plastic which suggests 1963 production year. The space for an (optional) radio is clearly visible in the centre of the dashboard, covered in textile and adorned with the inscription 'Škoda'. Column gear change is retained, but the wooden gear lever knob is non-standard. The engine temperature gauge right of the speedometer/odometer is also non-standard.*

starting the engine. As the engine could now be started by using the key only, the pull-out starter knob could be deleted. The pull-out choke was retained, the switches operating the wipers, heater, internal lighting and optional fog lights were now of the cradle type and the headlights were operated by a three-position switch: off, dipped beam and full beam. The three main dials – speedometer/odometer, fuel gauge and engine temperature gauge – were carried over from the earlier model. The two warning lights at the bottom of the speedometer also remained the same; they indicated the dynamo not charging the battery and low oil pressure.

The small glove box on the passenger side of the dashboard was enlarged and had a cover, the direction indicator stalk remained left of the steering column, but was now much shorter for safety and had an additional position for flashing the headlights, and all cars had a space in the dashboard for the optional radio. The upper side of the dashboard was covered in soft plastic and the lower edge in rubber from early 1963. Adjustment of the front seat backrests was easier as it could be done by turning a small plastic wheel rather than adjusting the retaining nut with a spanner. Octavias built in 1961 and most of 1962 still had a front bench seat with separate backrests, with completely separate front seats introduced in autumn 1962.

Late production cars from spring 1963 onwards had the same front seats as the Felicia (see Chapter 15), which were considerably more supportive and provided much better lateral support. A bed conversion was now standard. Traditional black rubber floormats were replaced with grey items while another minor but practical improvement was an additional position light and direction indicator atop the B-pillar,

*Octavia Super 1961 onwards, with a simplified radiator grille and fins on the rear wings. The inscription 'Super' just visible below the decorative side skirt on the front wing denotes the 1221cc engine. The external mirrors fitted to the wings and the decorative wheel trims are non-standard, the latter were often fitted to cars exported to Europe.*

also introduced in early 1963. Small hooks for clothes fitted to the inner side of the B-pillar was another nice touch introduced at the same time.

The choice of colours was slightly altered, and the following shades were available: white (now more common), light grey, beige, olive green, bright red, burgundy, green, brown, violet, dark blue and black. Notably, light blue was no longer offered, so this colour is typical of early Octavias. The last change of colours offered came in early 1963, when only violet, light grey and burgundy were retained from the previous choices. However, new colours were introduced, including dark grey, turquoise and blue-grey.

The system of Car Purchase Permits was abolished on 1 November 1962 and anyone could now buy an Octavia, although with a typical waiting time of several months. A deposit of 20,000 CZK had to be paid in advance, followed by the balance paid on taking delivery. The numerous references and forms related to the Car Purchase Permit (see Chapter 2) were no longer needed, which was a very positive development. Unfortunately, prices were still high; there was actually a significant hike, and a standard Octavia now cost 38,000 CZK, but a Super was not much more expensive at 39,500 CZK. In 1962-1963 this was an equivalent of about 25 average monthly salaries, which meant that updated Octavias were no more affordable than earlier models. In fact, the Octavia with the 1089cc engine was now less affordable than before. Some Octavias (including TS/1200 TS) were also sold by the state-owned Tuzex company on the 'free' market (without the need for the Car Purchase Permit) from 1961 onwards.

I will have to digress now and attempt to explain this rather alien concept to the British reader. Tuzex was set up by the Czechoslovakian Government in the late 1950s, the main purpose being for the state to obtain hard currency, the secondary purpose being to sell imported or quality domestic products to those Czechoslovakians who could afford them. The regime was desperate for hard currency so legislation was put in place making it illegal to have savings in any Western currency. The Czechoslovakians working abroad and paid in foreign currencies were obliged to exchange their surplus money for Tuzex crowns (*Tuzexové koruny,* TK in Czech). As can be expected, the exchange rate was set arbitrarily and heavily favoured the state. Those with a Tuzex account could then buy imported (or quality domestic) goods in Tuzex, but the system was wide open to corruption; it was possible to buy TK on the ubiquitous black market. I vaguely recall that the 'exchange rate' was some 5 CZK to 1 TK in the 1970s and 1980s, by which time the black market was quietly tolerated by the authorities. I am not sure what it was like in the 1960s.

The updated 1089cc Octavia had a total production of 173,279 units which makes it the main production model, and for the updated Octavia Super it was 55,432. Total production of all Octavias (including the early model) was 229,531 cars, the corresponding figure for the Super being 79,489. This gives a grand total of 309,020 two-door saloon Octavias, and all were built at the main plant in Mladá Boleslav. The last saloon Octavia, a grey Super, rolled off the production line on 11 April 1964. The Octavia was becoming obsolete by then, more about which later. It was the most produced Czechoslovakian car up to that date.

Octavias were very common in Czechoslovakia well into the 1970s and even early 1980s as regularly used family cars. They were mostly well maintained and their high quality ensured longevity. They have survived in substantial numbers (probably high thousands) and they are among the most popular classics in my old country today. This is helped by an excellent supply of spare parts: there is extensive secondary production mainly in the Czech Republic but also in Slovakia with the vast majority of parts being re-manufactured. Spartak owners also benefit as there are many interchangeable parts. The superb availability includes not only mechanical parts but also some body panels, although one notable exception is the windscreen which is difficult to come by. Overall, it is probably fair to say that spare parts supply for the Octavia in my old country is comparable to that of the Morris Minor or MGB/MGB GT in the UK.

CHAPTER 9

# OCTAVIA TS TYPE 995 AND 1200 TS TYPE 999 (1959-1964)

**TS STANDS** for Touring Sport and it denotes the 'hot' version of the Octavia. The colloquial Czech expression is 'Te-eska'. It was available with the same 1089cc engine as the TS, but the majority had the 1221cc engine and these were referred to as 1200 TS. Both engines had two Jikov carburettors similar to those used in standard Octavias, while modified camshafts made it possible to achieve higher rpm. Torque was 75Nm and 86Nm respectively.

The TS versions were considerably faster than standard Octavias, and like all saloon Octavias they were quicker in real life than their official top speed figures indicated. The TS could come close to 85mph (135km/h) and there are plausible stories of 1200 TSs briefly doing 88mph (140km/h). Cruising speed was around 69mph (110km/h) for both models. TSs and 1200 TSs also accelerated very well by the standards of their time, but their fuel economy was, understandably, worse than for standard Octavias. The 1089cc TS was marginally more economical but not by much. Technical specifications are given in Table 7.

Production probably started in early 1960, but some earliest TSs may have been built in late 1959; their numbers would have been very small, likely in low double figures. The TS was launched at the Geneva Motor Show in March 1960 and attracted much attention. The first 457 cars were of the 1959-60 model, except for the decorative 'propeller' never fitted to the TS, and the radiator grille was straight rather than concave; in fact, identical to that of early Felicias (see Chapter 15). It was, however, different to the grille fitted to standard 1961-on Octavias, while TS and later 1200 TS models had thicker vertical bars in their grilles.

The early cars had a twin-carburettor

TABLE 7

| **Škoda Octavia TS Type 995/Octavia 1200 TS Type 999 (1960-1962/1962-1964)** | |
|---|---|
| Length | 4065mm |
| Width | 1600mm |
| Height | 1430mm |
| Wheelbase | 2390mm |
| Kerb weight | 920kg/930kg |
| Bore x stroke | 68x75mm/72x75mm |
| Capacity | 1089cc/1221cc |
| Power | 50bhp/55bhp at 5500/5100rpm |
| Compression ratio | 8.4:1 |
| Top speed | 82mph (130km/h)/ 85mph (135km/h) * |
| Acceleration | 0-62mph (0-100km/h) 20/17 seconds |
| Average economy | 31mpg (9l/100km)/29.5mpg (9.5l/100km) |

**These are official figures. TS Octavias were in fact slightly quicker – see the text above.*

*Early TS with the 1089cc engine. Note the radiator grille without the decorative propeller, fog lights and optional wheel trim. White-walled tyres were also optional, mainly fitted to the TS and 1200 TS.*

1089cc engine, with the larger engine introduced in late 1961 and becoming standard from 1962. Early TSs had separate front seats, but still a column gear change, windscreen washers and two-tone horns were standard from the start. The only indication of the more powerful engine was a small inscription of 'Touring Sport' just below the decorative side skirts on the front wings and next to the rear registration plate. Colours available were the same as for standard Octavias.

The early TSs were mostly exported to Western Europe and only minuscule numbers were sold on the domestic 'free' market as their price of 42,000 CZK made them far from affordable. A TS was displayed at 'May Day Rally of the Working People' in Mladá Boleslav on 1 May 1960 as 'another success on our way to Communism'.

Cars made from January 1961 onwards corresponded to the 1961 model, complete with fins on the rear wings. In contrast to standard Octavias (and Supers) they had a floor gear change, with the gear lever atop the central tunnel, and completely separate front seats, now the same as fitted to Felicias. A black steering wheel was introduced at the same time together with a new speedometer calibrated to 160km/h (100mph). The larger engine was mostly fitted from late 1961 onwards. Total production was limited to 2273 cars. The proportion of TS vs 1200 TS is not entirely clear, but one source indicates 967 (including 457 of the early model) TS and 1306 1200 TS. Production effectively ended in 1963 with only eight of the 1200 TS model built in early 1964.

The vast majority of 'hot' Octavias built were exported, mainly to Sweden, Norway and other Western European countries, and, interestingly, small numbers were delivered to Bulgaria. Only a minority remained in Czechoslovakia, but they soon acquired cult status and an enthusiastic following. Because of their rarity, they are very sought after in my old country today, but unfortunately they are much rarer even

*1200 TS was something of a Q-car. The only identification was the small inscription 'Touring Sport' just below the decorative sideskirts on the front wings and to the right of the rear registration plate. (Courtesy Zdeněk Patera, www.auta5p.eu)*

than Felicias and almost impossible to find. If a TS or 1200 TS does turn up its price will be absurd, possibly close to 1,000,000 CZK (equivalent to some £33,000). On the plus side, there are very few TS-specific parts, so the few owners benefit from the excellent spare parts supply available to standard Octavia owners.

CHAPTER 10

# OCTAVIA IN MOTORSPORT

**SOMEWHAT SURPRISINGLY,** the Octavia played quite a significant role in motorsport in the 1960s. Its slightly sedate appearance was rather deceptive: the Octavia had handling, roadholding and reliability on its side, and another advantage was its optimal gearing, which made it possible to use the relatively limited power to maximum effect. It is fair to say that the designers struck the right balance between short and long gearing, thus achieving both decent acceleration and top speed. The Octavia never excelled in either respect, but it was good in both (by the standards of its time) and a tough opponent even for faster cars of its class. This particularly applied to TS models with twin-carburettor engines. The rally cars could be tuned for increased output, and figures given by various sources vary widely – between 65bhp and nearly 100bhp. Different levels of tuning were probably used for different purposes.

Interestingly, first successes in motorsport were achieved by standard single-carburettor Octavias and a Super (not TS) took part in the 1960 Rallye Monte-Carlo. Norwegian crew Edward Gjolberg and Jan Martinsen came second in the up to 1300cc class. There was also a factory team consisting of three crews: Josef Vidner-Jaroslav/Jaroslav Mansfeld, Miroslav Fousek/Oldřich Horsák, and Jaroslav Netušil/Jaroslav Bobek. Unfortunately, they were given too little time for preparation and their cars developed technical problems. As a result, they came in around the hundredth position out of the total of 297 cars.

I should probably explain that Rallye Monte-Carlo was a long-distance race in those days, starting in various capitals of Europe and converging on Monte Carlo. The Czechoslovakian crews started from the Polish capital Warsaw.

Another success was achieved in the rather exotic locations of Colombia and Venezuela, namely the Bogota-Caracas race. Venezuelan driver Sergio Vivaldi won the up to 1600cc class of production cars with a standard Octavia, not even an Octavia Super. Much of the race took place on very poor roads, but the Octavia performed faultlessly, and only 22 out of 63 cars completed the race, which shows how tough it must have been.

The social climate in Czechoslovakia was becoming more relaxed by 1960 and the regime now tolerated or indeed supported domestic car rallies and those within the Eastern Bloc. The first major rally after decades was Rally of Czechoslovakia in May 1960, which started and finished in two most famous Czech spa towns, Mariánské Lázně and Karlovy Vary respectively. The rally covered the whole territory of the Czechoslovakian Republic, including Moravia and Slovakia and the total distance was some 2500km (c1500 miles). Octavias were up against East German Wartburgs and Soviet Moskviches and they won convincingly. The (slightly unusual) up to 1150cc class was won by Vladimír Hubáček in a standard Octavia, and the crew of Horsák/Fousek driving a Super came first in the up to 1300cc class.

*Early model Super driven to victory by Václav Bobek and Jaroslav Mansfeld in the Moscow-Leningrad-Minsk-Warsaw-East Berlin-Prague in June 1960. The picture was presumably taken in East Berlin. The political slogan in German means 'For Universal and Complete Disarmament'. (Courtesy forum.skodahome.cz)*

The next major rally was organised by the Soviets, and took place in June 1960. The rally was named 'For Peace and Friendship' and the start took place in Moscow, on 4 June 1960. This was purely a rally of the 'Soviet Empire', with sixty crews from the USSR, Czechoslovakia, German Democratic Republic, Poland and Hungary taking part, and the route led via Leningrad (now St Petersburg), Minsk (now capital of Belarus), Warsaw and East Berlin to Prague. Because of the political aspects of the rally, the factory team was given sufficient time for preparation and it made all the difference. The crew of Václav Bobek/Jaroslav Mansfeld were the winners, followed by a highly competent East German crew (unfortunately I have not found their names) driving an underpowered Wartburg 311. Another Czechoslovakian crew of Miroslav Fousek/Oldřich Horsák took the third position. The Czechoslovakians were driving Octavia Supers.

They repeated their success in 1961 when the rally started in Prague and finished in Moscow. The crew of Zdeněk Mráz and Jaroslav Šustr were the winners, this time driving a TS. The 1962 rally started in Budapest and cars were divided into classes for the first time, and the crew of Miroslav Fousek/Viktor Krupička won the up to 1300cc class with their 1200 TS, thus achieving a Czechoslovakian hat-trick.

Octavias also performed well against European cars: the young and talented Zdeněk Mráz and Vojtěch Rieger won the up to 1300cc class in the Polish rally, called Rajd Polski, in September 1960. Their main opponent was the superb Polish rally driver Sobieslaw Zasada driving a Simca Aronde Monthléry, and after a long battle the Octavia Super (this was not a TS!) came out on top. To round off the eventful year of 1960, Zdeněk Mráz won the very first Rally Vltava with a standard Octavia (the rally was named after the Czech river flowing through Prague). Sadly, Zdeněk Mráz died after a fatal accident on a circuit near Prostějov, Moravia driving a racing special Střela 1100 (Czech for a missile) on 17 September 1961.

From 1961 onwards the faster TS and, more so, 1200 TS bore the brunt of the action. They were highly successful in rallies both domestic and international and honours from international events often went to Scandinavian drivers. The list of successes is long, but at least some should be mentioned here. The TS and 1200 TS achieved a hat-trick in Rallye Monte-Carlo, winning the up to 1300cc class in 1961, 1962 and 1963! Finnish drivers Esko Keinanen and Rainer Eklund came first in the up to 1300cc class in 1961, and their victory is made even more impressive by the fact that their car was an early TS, not a 1200 TS. Second in the class came Norwegians Edward Gjolberg and Jan Martinsen who repeated their 1960 success but this time in a 1200 TS. Esko Keinanen went on to win the up to 1300cc class in the Thousand Lakes Rally in his native Finland later that year.

The finest hour for the fast Octavia came at the 1962 Rallye Monte-Carlo. In their 1200 TS Esko Keinanen, then 26 years old but already highly experienced, and his co-driver/navigator Rainer Eklund, fought an epic battle with the team of three Alfa Romeo Giuliettas. The Alfas were faster in a straight line, but the crew's skills, as well as the roadholding and reliability of their Octavia

*The up to 1300cc class winners of the 1962 Rallye Monte-Carlo: Esko Keinanen and Rainer Eklund with their 1200 TS. (Courtesy Škoda archive, Mladá Boleslav, Czech Republic)*

proved decisive. The Finnish crew were the winners again, followed by the three Alfas, and another Finnish driver, Nils Eklund, came fifth. Esko Keinanen also repeated his 1961 class victory in the Thousand Lakes Rally in 1962, his main opponent on that occasion the famous Erik Carlsson driving a Saab 850 Sport.

The winner of the 1963 Rallye Monte-Carlo was Norwegian crew Edward Gjolberg and Carl Karlan with their 1200 TS. The Octavia could not be considered a truly modern car by then, but if properly handled could still perform extremely well, and these brilliant successes beg the question of why a factory team took part only in 1962. They were given very little time for training, just like in 1960 but, even so, Miroslav Fousek and Josef Vidner finished in a respectable tenth position. In fact, Škoda's factory team was prepared to take part in the 1963 Rallye Monte-Carlo, but a decision was made at a 'higher level' not to send the team to the rally. I freely admit that the reasons for such a bizarre decision are beyond me.

Octavias also performed well on the American continent. They took part in the Shell 4000 Rally across Canada in 1962, the number denoting its length in miles, and the start was in Montreal, Quebec with the finish in Vancouver, British Columbia. The route had to be covered in six days and went through some sparsely populated and rather inhospitable areas of Canada, meaning the crews had to carry strictly specified emergency equipment in case they got stranded. Reliability was of vital importance ... which favoured the Octavia. The Trans-Canada Rally, as it was also referred to, was probably the world's toughest long-distance rally at the time. Václav Bobek, by then an experienced rally driver, was working in Canada in spring 1962, his job to train staff of Škoda dealerships in Canada on various aspects of Octavia maintenance. When he learned about the rally he decided to take part, and this alone shows how much more relaxed the social climate in Czechoslovakia had become compared to the early 1950s. Bobek obtained consent from the Škoda management to use an Octavia Super and to find a Canadian navigator.

Such activities would have been unthinkable (and, if attempted, associated with huge personal risk) a few years earlier. Bobek found an excellent navigator, Mr Joe Mazuch, a Canadian with Czech ancestors. 62 cars set off from Montreal, but only 31 finished the rally, the Octavia arriving in a respectable 14th position, having experienced no technical problems. This was a promising start, but the 1964 rally brought much greater success. This time, the start was in Vancouver and the finish in Montreal.

Three Octavia 1200 TSs took part with the crews of Joe Mazuch (now as a driver)/ Harry Dodsworth, Václav Bobek/Jim Luce and Blair Bunch/Robin Edwards. The last-named crew performed best, winning the up to 1300cc class, the Bobek/Luce crew took silver in the same class and Joe Mazuch with Harry Dodsworth came fourth. The Octavias also won silver in the teams contest – the winners were the Swedes with their Volvos. Ironically, this great success was achieved in mid-April 1964 when production of saloon Octavias came to an end. Mazuch also took part in the 1965 rally – which once again started in Montreal and finished in Vancouver – and he and his navigator Paul Wilson drove a white 1200 TS and came second in the up to 1300cc class.

Even in 1963 when the Octavia was approaching obsolescence, the crew of Josef Vidner/Bohuslav Staněk won the up to 1300cc class on the Tour d'Europe and came fifth overall. Another success on the home front was the class victory and third position overall on the 1963 Rally Vltava 3, the successful crew being Jaroslav Bobek (brother of Václav Bobek) and Leo Hnatevič with their 1200 TS.

Some TS and 1200 TS models took part in local and regional rallies well into the

*Lada 1200, aka VAZ 2101, was a much more modern design than the Octavia, but did not perform very well against the 1200 TS. (Courtesy Zdeněk Patera, www.auta5p.eu)*

1970s. Interestingly, the regime tolerated car races and rallies and presented them as evidence of normal life. The Communist Party even introduced the term 'Normalisation'. From about 1972 onwards, the Octavias were often up against brand new Soviet Ladas (VAZ 2101), based on the Fiat 124, the 1967 Car of the Year. However, they were quite heavily modified to survive in Russian conditions, which made them tougher but also considerably heavier than the Italian originals. They were good cars, but the bombastic Soviet propaganda made them look brilliant, something which they could not live up to in real life. 1200 TSs held their own and mostly came out on top, which delighted Czechs and Slovaks because it was soon after the Soviet occupation of Czechoslovakia.

Much-vaunted Soviet cars of a new generation being outrun and outmanoeuvred by older Octavias was something most people just loved. Looking at the matter from the strictly technical point of view, such results were not that surprising. The slightly slower TS was at a disadvantage, but the 1200 TS had the same top speed and acceleration as the early Lada, and, while marginally less powerful, it was considerably lighter (by approximately 60kg), so that the power-to-weight ratio was slightly in the Octavia's favour. Independent suspension in the front and rear also gave the Octavia an edge (the Lada had a rigid live axle at the rear). Because of this and its ideal weight distribution, the 1200 TS was more manoeuvrable and also had better roadholding.

CHAPTER 11

# OCTAVIA COMBI TYPE 993C, TYPE 703C AND TYPE 704 (1961-1971)

**COMBI (OR KOMBI)** is Czech for an estate car, the colloquial Czech expression is *Kombík*. By the early 1960s the need arose for a car with the advantage of increased practicality and, in fact, an estate version of the Spartak was considered but never built, but things were very different with the Octavia.

As so often in my old country, much depended on the current political and

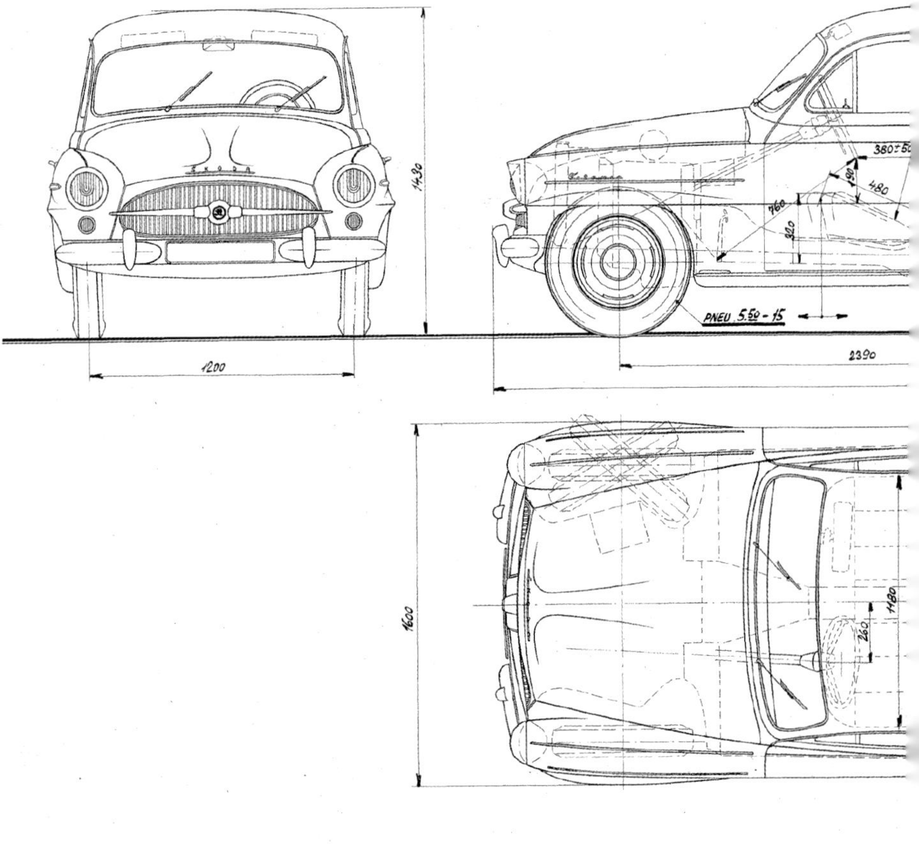

social climate although this was gradually improving since the mid-1950s. The regime was becoming less extreme, there were no political show trials and indeed, many political prisoners from the late 1940s and early 1950s were released long before serving their (unjustified) sentences in full. Some were even recognised not to be guilty of their alleged crimes. While Czechoslovakia was still far from being a democracy, the regime was much less oppressive than before. The economy was also improving with more consumer goods available, and although the standard of living was still lagging behind developed countries, the improvements compared to the early 1950s were noticeable.

Car ownership was increasing steadily, particularly since the Octavia was launched in early 1959. People were able to go on holidays, albeit mostly within Czechoslovakia or possibly in some countries of the Eastern Bloc and many families could afford a small cottage in the country. Such cottages were bought, or more often built on plots that could be purchased from the state, and numerous cottages surrounded many major Czechoslovakian cities, particularly Prague, Brno and Bratislava. The regime welcomed and encouraged this trend for its own reasons: people were kept relatively happy and, at the same time, out of the way over weekends. They were busy building or doing up their cottages and small adjacent

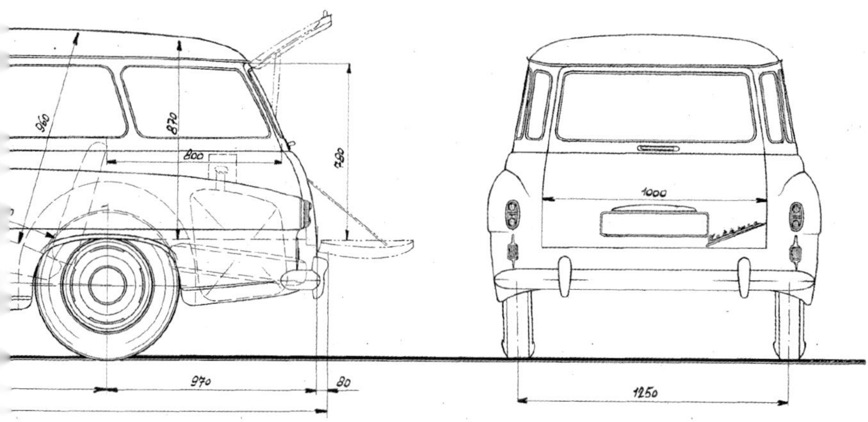


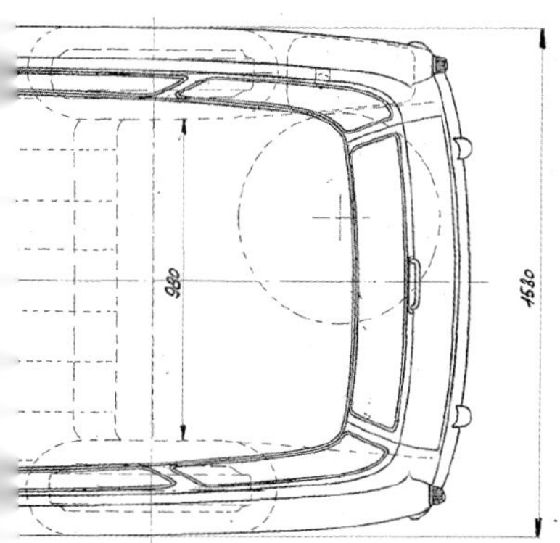


*Drawing of the very first prototype of Octavia Combi from 1959. Note the decorative propeller on the radiator grille and the absence of the fins.*

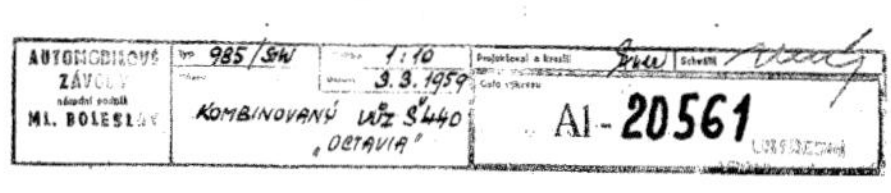

gardens which made them less likely to cause trouble for the regime.

From the mid-1960s onwards it became more common to build even family homes for permanent residence, particularly in smaller towns, but also on the outskirts of larger cities.

The need for an estate car was recognised in 1959, and Škoda was asked to come up with a solution. It was clear from the start that the way forward would be a small family estate based on the successful Octavia.

The first prototype of the estate version was built as early as summer 1959, based on the early model of the Octavia. It had smart two-tone paint, not normally used on Octavias. A further five prototypes followed in 1960 and these already had the simplified radiator grille and fins on the rear wings as fitted to the 1961-on saloons. The dashboard was also identical to the 1961-on model – in fact, the new layout was first tried out on the Combi prototypes.

The column gear change was retained, as was the gearbox itself, and there was synchromesh on all gears bar first. The umbrella handle-shaped hand brake was in the same position as before, to the left of the steering column (in the standard left-hand-drive cars). The fuel tank was placed behind the right-hand side rear wheelarch, and had the same 30-litre capacity as saloon Octavias, and there was space for a 20-litre jerry can behind the left-hand side wheelarch, which improved the range significantly. The rear bench seat could be folded flat to create a load area 1495mm long and up to 1355mm wide, and the minimum width between the rear wheelarches was 980mm.

The prototypes were successfully tested and the Combi went into production with minimal alterations in July 1961. It was generally similar to the 1961-on model up to the B-pillar, and the boot was considerably more spacious at 690 litres with the seats up and loaded to the roof. With the seats down the maximum capacity (again loaded to the roof) increased to 1050 litres. The tailgate was split, with the lower part hinged at the bottom of the opening, rather like on some high-end estates of today, and the spare wheel was now under the floor of the boot, accessible via a separate bottom-hinged door.

Like all Octavias, Combis were two-door, which was something of a disadvantage in an estate. The external dimensions were the same as for standard Octavias, as was the wheelbase, and the larger, later engine with 1221cc and 47bhp was standard. This made sense, because the Combi was significantly heavier than the saloon, with a typical kerb weight of 950-960kg. I had the opportunity to drive a well-maintained Combi over quite a long distance a few years ago, and while more powerful than my 1089cc Octavia it still felt less agile.

However, official performance figures for a Combi were identical to the Octavia Super. One of the prototypes achieved a top speed of 76.3mph (122km/h), but that was exceptional – figures of 72-75mph (115-120km/h) were more realistic. The economy was slightly worse, typically 31-35mpg (8-9l/100km) and I have not found specific acceleration figures for the early Combi, but with their extra weight they probably accelerated slightly slower than standard Octavias. The Combi was as well built and reliable as a standard Octavia and the much improved carrying capacity (400kg compared to 350kg) came in handy. The steering, brakes and suspension were the same as the standard Octavias, the only exception being a stronger transverse leaf spring at the rear to cope with increased loads. The weight distribution of 46:54 front to rear was marginally worse compared to the saloon, but still decent, which meant that the good handling and roadholding were largely retained.

As the main plant in Mladá Boleslav was busy producing saloon Octavias, Combis were built exclusively in the Kvasiny plant in Eastern Bohemia. Initial production was slow: only 502 cars were built between July 1961 and the end of the year, and production

*An early Octavia Combi with fins on the rear wings and somewhat superfluous Combi inscriptions just under the decorative sideskirts on the front wings.*

was always much slower compared to saloons, and never reached 6000 cars per year. The highest annual output, of 5850 Combis, was achieved in 1965, by which time production of saloons had ended.

Various improvements were introduced during the long production run. In common with the saloon version, the upper side of the dashboard was covered in soft plastic and the lower edge in rubber from 1963. An external rear view mirror on the driver's side, so far an aftermarket option for all Octavias, became standard in January 1965, and windscreen washers were introduced at the same time, together with a black steering wheel.

One major innovation was moving the gear lever on top of the central tunnel, the same arrangement as the Octavia TS/1200 TS and Felicias. The central tunnel was now covered in a medium-grey carpet with sound insulation underneath. The proportion of plastic parts in the interior was increasing steadily from the mid-1960s onwards, and armrests on the doors were introduced later in 1965 and became standard in 1966. The internal rear-view mirror and both sun visors were now the same as in the Škoda 1000 MB (see Chapter 16) and were larger than original items. The load area was carpeted, and the carpet could be removed for cleaning.

The overall design of the Octavia was visibly ageing by the mid-1960s. This was recognised and several proposals for modernisation of the Combi were put forward in 1965-1966, some proposing only very superficial alterations, others more courageous. However, all such proposals involved alterations to the bodywork only, and even then, the two-door layout, limiting practicality of any estate car, was to be retained. No changes to the engine, chassis and all mechanical parts were proposed.

Another model, namely a Combi-based Octavia van, was introduced in 1967, albeit for export only, mainly to Denmark, Norway, Sweden, but also Portugal. While moderately practical and highly reliable, this version

*The Octavia van was a minor, if interesting, episode in the Octavia story. They are extremely rare in Europe and, to my knowledge, non-existent in the Czech Republic or Slovakia.*

did not really catch on, and production was limited to a few hundred units. I have not succeeded in finding the accurate figure.

The 1968 model referred to as Type 703C was first shown at the Brno Motor and Engineering Show in September 1967. Comments were positive, but it was recognised that the Octavia was an ageing design by now. Production started in the Kvasiny plant in January 1968, and this model had a simplified radiator grille with nine straight horizontal bars, and therer were additional direction indicators on the front wings. The umbrella type handbrake lever, until then placed under the dashboard to the left of the driver, was replaced with a more modern stick-shaped item, and moved to the central tunnel behind the gear lever.

Fittings for seatbelts on front seats were also added, and the seatbelts themselves became standard from 1 January 1969, the day that seatbelts on new cars became a legal requirement in Czechoslovakia. The seats themselves were slightly altered to provide better lateral support, and the bench rear seat was replaced with two seats that could be folded separately, which improved versatility. A bed conversion remained standard. The traditional fins on the rear wings were retained, emphasising the age of the design. The same applied to the padded dashboard with the three circular dials, unchanged since 1963, while the traditional bumper overriders were replaced with rubber items.

The last facelift took place in the summer of 1969; these cars were designated Type 704. New horizontal tail lights from the 1969-on Škoda 100/110 (successor to the 1000 MB) were introduced, and the by-then somewhat archaic fins were deleted. Like in previous Octavias the seats could be completely reclined for sleeping, as standard. The dashboard originating from the Škoda 1000 MB (see Chapter 16) was

*Original picture of the completely different 1969-on cabin. Note the two-spoke steering wheel without the traditional inner ring, and the new dashboard, both the same as fitted to the Škoda 1000 MB. The somewhat incongruous-looking heater, visible under the dashboard, is carried over from earlier Octavias. To me, the overall impression is one of a futile attempt to update a design that was well past its best. (Courtesy Autorevue.cz)*

more modern-looking, but also safer due to increased use of soft plastics.

The compression ratio of the 1221cc engine was increased to 7.8:1, which increased power to 51bhp.

The attempt to improve the Octavia's performance was not a success, however, the improvements in speed and acceleration being minimal, as the last Combi was marginally heavier than its predecessors; tipping the scales at 970kg. The official figure for top speed was now 78mph (125km/h), which was rather optimistic (unlike figures for saloon Octavias) and in real life these last Combis could briefly just top 75mph (120km/h). Their 0-62mph (0-100km/h) time in seconds remained in the high 20s, largely the same as for the original 1959 saloon models with 1089cc engines. This was not the performance expected from a modern small family estate in the late 1960s or even early 1970s.

Cars built from 1970 onwards had either half-or full imitation leather seats. One handy feature was a small switch for switching out the ignition. This was hidden under the dashboard and not easy to find if you weren't in the know, thus making this model harder to steal. Such minor improvements increased practicality, comfort and security, but they could not disguise the fact that development potential of the Octavia was at its end.

There was speculation in the Czechoslovakian motoring press in 1969-1970 about possible replacement of front drum brakes with discs and the introduction

*Octavia Combi of the last production model (1969-on). Note absent fins and the horizontal rear lights from the Škoda 100/110. Even the dashboard was from the Škoda 1000 MB. Many Octavia fans would say that this is no longer a 'proper' Octavia. I don't disagree with them ...*

of fittings for rear seat belts, but these improvements did not materialise. They would have improved safety, but could not have significantly prolonged the Octavia's design life.

Probably because of slow production, the Combi was always expensive for what it offered. Prices started at 42,000 CZK in 1961, then were increased to 43,000 CZK in 1964 and to 44,500 CZK in 1965. The trend continued as the Combi was offered for 45,650 CZK in the spring of 1969. The final, and significant, price hike came in early 1970, when the price reached a rather absurd 62,000 CZK, the equivalent of just over 31(!) average monthly salaries. This could not be described as good value by any stretch of the imagination. The Combi was also sold in Tuzex (see Chapter 8) from 1965 onwards, and the initial price was 10,500 TK in 1965. Prices in Tuzex were rising more slowly, and the figure for a 1970 model with full imitation leather seats was 10,650 TK

While standard Octavias were phased out by April 1964, the Combi soldiered on until December 1971. The last of 54,086 Combis left the plant at Kvasiny on 17 December 1971, although an alternative source gives the total figure of 50,244. Some 500 replacement bodies for Combis were made in the Kvasiny plant until 1973, and the total production of all Octavia models exceeded 360,000 cars.

As much as I like the Octavia, I must say that it was outdated by the mid-1960s. By the early 1970s it was a relic from a bygone era, and should have been replaced years before.

CHAPTER 12

# THE OCTAVIA ABROAD

**THE OCTAVIA** was a great export success from the very start of its career in early 1959. While outwardly similar to the outgoing (and commercially successful) Spartak, the Octavia represented a major improvement over its predecessor. Ride and handling were much better, and the Octavia was also more agile while retaining good fuel economy. Build quality and, above all, quality of materials used improved significantly, so it is probably fair to say that the Octavia was one of the best small family cars anywhere in 1959.

The export success was also helped by the generally high standard of Škoda dealerships and good supply of spare parts, although, as in the case of the Spartak, this was sometimes at the expense of the domestic market. In contrast to the Spartak, the Octavia was never offered in two-tone paint, which in my view is rather unfortunate.

Czechoslovakian state-owned vehicle export company Motokov successfully exported Octavias to many countries. Nearly 15,000 were exported during 1959, the first year of production, which was almost a third of all Octavias built in that year.

The export success of the Spartak had also resulted in shortages on the domestic 'market', and, as a result, the Car Purchase Permit system had to remain in place.

The main export destination in 1959 was Belgium, with 2700 cars delivered. Octavias were assembled in Belgium from parts delivered from Czechoslovakia. Belgian production took place in Ghent, while East Germany bought 2000 Octavias and West Germany 1500.

Substantial deliveries also headed to Finland and Norway, traditional Škoda customers, as tough and reliable Octavias performed well in Scandinavian conditions. About 1000 cars were exported to Poland, and similar numbers went to The Netherlands. The relative success of the Spartak on the US market was repeated, with 600 Octavias delivered that year, and, interestingly, 450 cars were delivered to Venezuela. Small numbers went to other exotic locations such as Brazil, Mexico, Cuba, African countries such as Guinea and Mozambique, and even to New Zealand.

The early Octavias continued to do well in 1960, with similar numbers to 1959 exported, but, as production was increasing steadily, there were more cars available for the domestic market.

The UK became an important export market, assembly of Octavias in Belgium continued and was joined by assembly in the Republic of Ireland. Standard models made up some two thirds of exported cars, the other third was Supers. The TS model joined in from the spring of 1960, although single cars may have been exported in late 1959. The numbers of TS Octavias were very small; I could not find the accurate figure, but it can be safely assumed that some 400 out of the total of 457 built in 1960 were exported. The main destinations for the 'hot' early Octavias were Austria, Denmark, Switzerland and West Germany, and, interestingly, some were also delivered to Morocco.

*The advertisement for the Octavia as published in The Motor, 26 October 1960. The figures for top speed and fuel economy, 80mph (128km/h) and 40mpg respectively, are somewhat optimistic. Realistic figures would have been 75mph (120km/h) and 37mpg. (Courtesy Marc Lawrence private archive).*

Exports increased to nearly 30,000 Octavias, including 9000 Supers, in 1961, and almost all were the updated 1961 model. The main customer was Finland, which bought 4000, and East Germany followed closely with 3900 with significant numbers exported to Belgium (locally assembled), The Netherlands, and, for the first time, the UK. Exports to West Germany also continued successfully, even though there were no diplomatic relations between Czechoslovakia and West Germany at the time(!). Smaller deliveries went to Austria and Denmark, and many Octavias were delivered to Eastern Bloc countries such as Bulgaria, Hungary and Poland. Limited numbers of updated models were even exported to Australia, New Zealand and Japan. Exports of the TS model increased rapidly, even though the overall numbers remained very small, the main export markets being Sweden (111 cars) and Norway (72).

The success of the Spartak and early Octavia in the US was not repeated in 1961, and indeed, exports to the US all but collapsed, with a mere 30 sold. I have not found any clear explanation for this, but one speculative explanation is that politics may have interfered as this was the year of the Berlin Crisis, which began in spring 1961. Then the Berlin Wall was built by East Germany (on orders of the Soviets) in August 1961, and the world came to the brink of World War 3. In particular, the Soviet attitude appeared utterly irresponsible, which antagonised the West and led to a sharp rise of anti-Communism. The anti-Communist mood was most marked in the US, and Americans became reluctant to buy any products originating from Communist-led countries. The Cuban missile crisis followed in 1962 and, once again the world was on the brink of total disaster. It is possible that these events had a bearing on customer preferences particularly in the US and, to a lesser extent, in Canada.

However, export of Octavias to European countries continued successfully in 1962, 1963 and 1964, and the numbers of cars exported in 1962 and 1963 were similar to those in 1961. They dropped sharply in 1964 as production of the Octavia in saloon guise came to an end in April of that year. 1962 saw start of licensed production in Ceylon (now Sri Lanka). Octavias were assembled in Colombo from parts delivered from Czechoslovakia and with Czechoslovakian technical support. Total production is not known, but it is estimated that some 50 cars were assembled each month until early 1964. Their quality was considered very good, close to their Czechoslovakian-built counterparts.

Pricing placed the Octavia close to the class average on most export markets. Unlike later Škodas from the 1970s and particularly 1980s it was not the cheapest car on the market, but it was by no means expensive, and offered good value.

The Octavia Combi was exported from 1961. The initial production was slow, but deliveries (and exports) increased steadily with rising production from 1962 onwards, and, typically up to two thirds of Combis were exported each year. The best year was 1966, by which time the Combi was the only Octavia model still in production. From 5295 Combis built that year only 1465 remained in Czechoslovakia, and 3830 (72%) were exported. However, the Octavia (now only in Combi guise) was becoming progressively less competitive from the mid-1960s onwards. Like the saloon model from 1963-on, the Combi was now outclassed by much more modern competitors, such as the Ford Cortina and Simca 1300, in this case their estate versions.

The Combi-based Octavia van was exported to Denmark, Norway, Portugal and Sweden from 1966 to 1968, but export figures for standard Combis were declining steadily. In 1967 the UK bought 264, Belgium 207 and Norway 195, and Iceland bought 80. Larger deliveries were made to Eastern Bloc countries such as

East Germany (915) and Hungary (452) where the Octavia was still competitive. Interestingly, 1967 saw the start of licensed production in Chile, the local company, IMCODA, assembling Combis from parts delivered from Czechoslovakia.

With Czechoslovakian technical support in place the proportion of Chilean manufactured components was rising steadily from 1968 onwards, with bodies built locally from summer 1968. The cars were of the 1965-1967 model with fins on the rear wings and circular dials. The conditions were somewhat makeshift, though, and minor local modifications were made. These were aimed at simplifying production, as the workforce was inexperienced, and one example was the simplified radiator grille made of strong wire mesh. As far as can be established, Chilean Combis performed well, often as farmers' vehicles or delivery vans. Total production is unclear: according to various sources it was c400 units or possibly up to 1000 built until 1971.

CHAPTER 13

# HOW DID THE OCTAVIA COMPARE?

**IN CONTRAST** to most cars from the Eastern Bloc the Octavia was fully competitive against Western European small family cars of its time. Its abilities were well recognised, and it was always seen as a serious contender. The much later Škoda jokes certainly did not apply to the Octavia! In many ways it was right up there with the best of its class, and this was certainly the case from 1959 until early 1963 when the new generation of small family cars made its appearance.

As with the Spartak, it is probably appropriate to make a separate comparison with Eastern European cars and cars from Western Europe. However, it should be said that while the 'Soviet Empire' was already lagging behind Europe in terms of civilian design, technology and production, the gap was considerably smaller in 1960 than later. The technical lead of the West only became significant in the mid-1960s, and striking by the mid-1970s. By the early 1980s the gap was enormous, and was increasing steadily.

The main Soviet competitor was the Moskvich 407, an almost exact contemporary of the Octavia. This was the successor of the earlier 402, which had competed against the Spartak. Well, I am talking about competition for the want of a better word. Both Czechoslovakian and Soviet cars were initially sold under the Car Purchase Permit system. Production of this model started in the Moscow factory of AZLK (Automobile Factory of Lenin's Komsomol. Avtomobilnyi Zavod Leninskovo Komsomola in Russian) in late 1958, and continued until late 1963.

The Moskvich had two advantages over its Czechoslovakian counterpart: it was a four-door saloon, and was available in a smart two-tone paint. Even so, the Octavia was clearly superior in most respects. The Moskvich had a larger 1357cc engine of OHV layout but with a similar output of 45bhp, while the gearbox was a three-speeder with column gear change, replaced by a four-speeder towards the end of production. The top two gears were synchronised in either case, although this did not compare favourably with the Octavia's four-speed gearbox with synchromesh on all gears bar first.

The Moskvich had independent front suspension but a beam-type live axle at the rear. The high centre of gravity (at 1560mm, it was 130mm taller than the Octavia) did not help handling either. The 407 was significantly heavier than the Octavia, weighing in at 990kg, and as a result it was severely underpowered, even by the standards of the early 1960s. Acceleration was very slow, 0-62mph (0-100km/h) taking at least 36 seconds, while top speed was given as 72mph (115km/h) or, according to a different source, 75mph (120km/h), much the same as for the Octavia. However, the Octavia could get from standstill to 62mph (100km/h) some eight seconds quicker, and the Super could probably perform the same ten seconds quicker. Any Octavia had a vastly better power-to-weight ratio, roadholding and handling, and the Octavia was also better built and a clear winner in terms of fuel economy. The Moskvich struggled to

*Moskvich 407: reliable but heavy, thirsty and cumbersome. The two-tone paint is very smart though. (Courtesy Zdeněk Patera, www.auta5p.eu)*

return 28mpg (10l/100km) while the Octavia typically achieved 35-37mpg (7.6-8l/100km) in mixed driving.

I have found the price of the 407 in Czechoslovakia: they were sold for 31,000 CZK, an equivalent of nearly 24 average monthly salaries in 1960. This made the Moskvich more expensive than the standard Octavia but cheaper than the Super, and in my view, the higher price of the Moskvich compared to the Octavia was hard to justify.

As with the Octavia, no Car Purchase Permit was needed to buy a Moskvich from autumn 1962 onwards. For the modern-day enthusiast, the Moskvich could be an interesting choice. Unfortunately, the current political situation probably makes spare parts supply almost impossible.

Another competitor also imported into Czechoslovakia (and sold under the Car Purchase Permit scheme until autumn 1962) was the Wartburg 311 from East Germany. Unfortunately, I have not succeeded in finding the price of a 311 in Czechoslovakia. This model had competed with the Spartak as described on page 35, but in its original form it was even more inferior to the Octavia than to its predecessor. However, the original 311 was replaced by the updated 311/1000 in early 1962, the main difference being a more powerful engine: a two-stroke 992cc three-cylinder with 40bhp, later 45bhp. This made the Wartburg less underpowered than before, and matters improved further when the manufacturer succeeded in reducing the kerb weight from 960kg to 920kg in 1963.

The updated 311 was only marginally heavier than the Octavia, and the power was now comparable. Top speed was given as 72mph (115km/h), then 78mph (125km/h) from 1963. Both figures sound somewhat optimistic, indeed modern German sources (Wikipedia, German edition) give a more realistic 70mph (112km/h) and 72mph (115km/h) respectively. Acceleration figures are hard to come by, but I have found 27.5 seconds for the 0-62mph (0-100km/h) sprint – this relates to the lighter 1963-onwards

*Early (1962) Wartburg 311/1000: quite spacious but somewhat underpowered. (Courtesy Zdeněk Patera, www.auta5p.eu)*

model. The modernised 311 retained the four-door layout which made access to rear seats easy and gave it an edge over the Octavia in terms of practicality. Build quality was good, approaching that of the Octavia.

Even the 311/1000 still had transverse leaf spring front suspension and a beam-type rear axle, also with a transverse leaf spring.

Due to its more advanced all-independent suspension, the Octavia had an edge in handling. It could probably accelerate better than any pre-1963 Wartburg, and was certainly more economical. The 311/1000 typically returned around 30mpg (9.3l/100km) versus the Octavia's 35-37mpg (7.6-8l/100km) in mixed driving.

Like the Octavia, the Wartburg was available as an estate, referred to as the 311 Tourist, the estate significantly heavier and slower than the saloon model. Built in small numbers, it was not imported into Czechoslovakia.

The Polish competitors, the Syrena 101 and, from 1962 Syrena 102, were not imported into Czechoslovakia, so they competed against the Octavia in Poland only. Interestingly, the latter was the first Syrena with an all-metal body and no supporting ash frame, but still featuring rear-hinged 'suicide doors'. Both models had the 744cc two-stroke two-cylinder engine now uprated to 30bhp, although this was still inadequate even though kerb weight was reduced to 920kg. Top speed was now 66mph (105km/h), but I have not found acceleration figures, while fuel economy was similar to the Syrena 100 at some 33mpg (8.5l/100km).

The 102 was re-engined in 1963 when a 992cc Wartburg three-cylinder was fitted to a small number of cars designated 102S. With 40bhp on tap, these were reported to achieve 75mph (120km/h) with only marginally worse fuel economy. All Syrenas were two-door saloons, and like its predecessor the Spartak, the Octavia had a clear edge over all other small family cars from the Eastern Bloc. While it lost

*Syrena 102 was the weakest of all Octavia's competitors, losing out in every respect.*

*Morris Minor 1000, 1960 four-door model seen at a classic car show.*
*(Courtesy Zdeněk Patera, www.auta5p.eu)*

some points because of its two-door only layout, its build quality, reliability, handling, performance and economy made it a clear winner.

Cars from Western Europe represented a much more serious challenge, but the Octavia rose to it well. In the UK, its main competitors were the Morris Minor 1000, Ford Popular 100E and Anglia 105E, but also the formidable Triumph Herald. The Anglia 105E was the only one imported into Czechoslovakia.

The Minor competing with the Octavia was the 1000 model introduced in 1956 with a 948cc straight-four A-series engine offering 37bhp. This was upgraded to 1098cc and 48bhp in 1962. The Minor was designed by the famous Alec Issigonis (later Sir Alec Issigonis) during the latter part of WW2 and went into production in 1948, and despite its somewhat old-fashioned appearance, it was extremely advanced for its time, with all-independent suspension, rack-and-pinion steering and monocoque body. In fact, it was technically more advanced than the newer Octavia regarding the steering and body. With a 3759mm length and 2184mm wheelbase the Minor was smaller than the Octavia and it was also c125kg lighter, tipping the scales at 775kg. Top speed was similar at 75mph (120km/h) but acceleration was slower, with a 0-60mph (0-97km/h) time of 31.3 seconds.

The more powerful 1098cc Minor was quicker: its top speed was 77mph (124km/h), which made it marginally faster than the Octavia. The 0-60mph (0-97km/h) time was given as 24.8 seconds. It can be safely assumed that the 0-62mph (0-100km/h) time was similar to that of the Octavia, and fuel economy for both cars was also similar. The Octavia offered slightly more interior space and a larger boot, but on the other hand, the Minor offered the option of a four-door saloon, and this was its main advantage over the Octavia.

Both cars were also available as estates. In my view, the 'woodie' Traveller was as practical as and better-looking than the Octavia Combi, but overall, the Octavia and its British counterpart were evenly matched.

The two small family Fords were very different. The Popular 100E was an entry level version of the 100E Anglia (see Chapter 2) which had been in production until 1959. Production of the two-door only Popular 100E continued until 1962, which makes it a contemporary of the Octavia. The main drawback of the Popular 100E was its ancient 1172cc SV engine of pre-war design offering 36bhp and relatively poor fuel economy. The engine was not renowned for its longevity, and often needed a rebuild at around 60,000 miles (97,000km), less than half the Octavia engine's lifespan, and servicing every 1000 miles (1600km) was required. Again, this was about half the service interval recommended for the Octavia. The three-speed gearbox was another performance-limiting factor. Top speed was given at 69.9mph (111.8km/h) when tested by *Motor* magazine, but I have not found accurate acceleration figures, only estimates of the 0-60mph (0-97km/h) time varying between 32 and 37 seconds. This sounds realistic, but I am not in a good position to comment. Fuel economy was actually better than for the Anglia 100E at 33.2mpg (c8.5l/100km), but still not as good as for the Octavia. Overall, the Popular 100E was at a disadvantage.

The Anglia 105E launched in 1959 was a much tougher competitor, this model introducing completely new US-inspired styling complete with a reverse-rake rear window. Another major change was the new 997cc OHV straight-four offering 39bhp. The 105E shared the Octavia's two-door layout, but was slightly smaller at 3912mm in length, and both width and height were the same at 1422mm, and it was also lighter at 737kg. As a result, the 105E had top speed and acceleration similar to the more powerful Octavia with the *Motor* magazine test showing 74.3mph (118.8km/h) and a 0-60mph (0-97km/h) time of 26.9 seconds.

As one of the few small family cars of the time, the Anglia 105E was more economical

*Superbly maintained Ford Popular 100E. This smart-looking car was severely limited by its SV engine of pre-war design. (Photograph by Charles 01, licensed under CC 3.0 via Wikimedia Commons)*

*Ford Anglia 105E in De Luxe version, resplendent in two-tone paint. What a shame Octavias did not have this option! (Courtesy Zdeněk Patera, www.auta5p.eu)*

*Triumph Herald 1200: evenly matched with the Octavia ... and better-looking in that smart two-tone paint. (Photograph by Charles01, licensed under CC 3.0 via Wikimedia Commons)*

than its Czechoslovakian counterpart: on average it could achieve in excess of 40mpg (less than 7l/100km). The weak and problematic vacuum wipers of earlier Anglias were at last replaced by electric items, as featured on both the Minor and Octavia, and a heater was now fitted to the majority of cars, and later became standard. The 105E was joined by the Anglia 123E (aka Anglia Super) in late 1962, and this had a more powerful 1198cc engine also fitted to the early Cortina Mk 1. The 1.2-litre engine offered 46bhp, and top speed was about 78mph (125km/h) although this engine was much less durable than the 997cc version. The reason given by some sources was the flywheel, which was too heavy. Both the 105E and 123E were available in estate form with three doors.

Interestingly, small numbers of 105Es were imported into Czechoslovakia and sold under the Car Purchase Permit scheme in 1960-1961. While a little less spacious, they were (rightly in my view) considered closely matched with Octavias. Being Western and, therefore 'posh', some were probably allocated to moderately distinguished Comrades, but not quite deserving of a big Soviet Volga M21 or a Hillman Minx, both of which were imported in the early 1960s!

In my opinion, the most formidable British competitor to the Octavia was the Triumph Herald, also launched in 1959. The earliest 948cc cars were somewhat underpowered, but the 1147cc engine introduced in April 1961 resolved the problem. Compared to the Octavia, the Herald was slightly smaller but significantly lighter, tipping the scales at a mere 725kg (convertible) or 760kg (saloon). Even the estate weighing in at 860kg was some 40kg lighter than a saloon Octavia and nearly 100kg lighter than the Combi, yet in contrast to the Minor, Popular and Anglia, it had a separate chassis like the Octavia.

All Heralds bar three-door estates had two doors. With its 1147cc 39bhp engine the Herald had a better power-to-weight ratio than the Octavia, making it slightly faster, with a top speed of 78mph (125km/h). The Triumph was also noticeably more agile, with quicker acceleration, particularly in the lower speed range, the 0-60mph (0-97km/h) sprint typically taking around 23 seconds. Thanks in part to its rack-and-pinion steering, the

Herald had sporty handling and a famously tight turning circle (25ft or 7.6m!), which the Octavia had no chance of matching. The Herald's edge in agility increased further when the uprated 1147cc 51bhp 12/50 model was introduced in early 1963. While devoid of the lovely wooden dashboard fitted to some Heralds, the Octavia scored on build quality, longevity and slightly more spacious interior. Somewhat surprisingly, it was also more economical, returning 35-37mpg (7.6-8l/100km) in mixed driving versus the Herald's 31-35mpg (8-9l/100km), and this was probably on account of the Octavia's lower-revving engine.

The choice between the two cars was purely a matter of personal preference. For those preferring sporty handling and agility the Herald was the winner, while the Octavia appealed as a sturdy, more spacious (if still small) family car. Both were also available on the UK market in three-door estate form. The early model of the Octavia cost £745 in 1960 and the Herald was priced similarly, which made sense given how evenly matched the cars were.

The Octavia held its own equally well against continental European competitors. The Czechoslovakian car was more powerful, spacious and comfortable than the VW Beetle of 1960. The Beetle was the most common small family car in what was then West Germany, and it went on to become the most produced car of all time, mainly because of its simplicity, reliability and good economy. In terms of size, it was very similar to the Octavia, and, like the Octavia, the Beetle had a separate chassis and was available in two-door form only. In contrast to the Octavia, it was also available as a convertible, built in relatively limited numbers. The Beetle was basically a pre-war design with the air-cooled engine in the rear.

Production started in earnest soon after WW2, and while very advanced for its time, the Beetle was ageing by the early 1960s. This was manifesting itself particularly in poor aerodynamics (the coefficient of drag was 0.46), but also relatively confined space for passengers and a small boot, much of which was taken up by the spare wheel and battery. Other outdated features were a non-synchromesh gearbox and mechanical brakes, both replaced in 1962. The very pre-war style running boards were retained throughout the production run. As the Beetle was lighter than the Octavia, typically c840kg, its short-stroke 1192cc air-cooled flat-four offering 34bhp was sufficient for a top speed of 72mph (115km/h), ie close to that of the Octavia, but its acceleration was slower with 0-62mph (0-100km/h) taking about 33 seconds. On the plus side, it was just as well built as the Octavia and easily as reliable, and fuel economy was also similar.

Another West German competitor was the Ford Taunus 12M of 1959-1962. This was a very good looking car but, like the Octavia, was only available with two doors. It was one of the first German cars of monocoque construction, and was almost exactly the same length and width as the Octavia, but 90mm taller at 1520mm. Its kerb weight was also similar. The 12M was limited by its pre-war engine, the 1172cc straight-four of SV layout, also fitted to the Ford Popular 100E (and Anglia 100E) in the UK tuned to offer 38bhp rather than 36bhp as in the British Fords.

The majority of 12Ms had a three-speed gearbox, although some cars had a four-speed gearbox, their proportion on the production lines increasing from 1960 onwards. The 12M had a top speed of 69mph (110km/h) and slow acceleration, the 'sprint' from 0 to 62mph (0-100km/h) taking 37.5 seconds, some 10 seconds slower than the Octavia. Another disadvantage was less advanced suspension, with a rear beam-type axle and longitudinal leaf springs (the Beetle had all-independent suspension just like the Octavia). The ancient SV engine also adversely affected the fuel economy: typical average was some 32mpg (8.75l/100km).

The new, completely unrelated Taunus 12M launched in late 1962 was technically interesting, with a new 1183cc V4 engine driving the front wheels, the first time for a

*The main German competitor: Volkswagen Beetle. This is a 1960 model. (Courtesy Zdeněk Patera, www.auta5p.eu)*

*Ford Taunus 12M, 1959-1962 model: great looking (yes, it's that lovely two-tone paint yet again!) but let down by its prehistoric engine. (Courtesy Zdeněk Patera, www.auta5p.eu).*

Ford. The engine was relatively low-powered at 40bhp but this 12M was evenly matched with the Octavia in most respects and possibly slightly faster with a top speed of 76mph (122km/h). The acceleration was marginally slower, however, with 0-62mph (0-100km/h) taking a touch over 30 seconds. As an additional advantage, the new 12M was also available as a four-door saloon. Overall, it might have had a slight edge, but a much smaller one than the Ford Cortina or Simca 1300 (see later). Czechoslovakia did not import West German cars, possibly as part of an agreement with East Germany but, interestingly, Octavias were sold in West Germany.

The main French contenders were the Simca Aronde and Elysée, the former having been in production from 1951 and subject to many upgrades. The Octavia was up against the 1955-1960 model. The Aronde was slightly longer and taller but narrower than the Octavia, with a length, width and height of 4115mm, 1558mm and 1446mm respectively. The vast majority of Arondes had the advantage of a four-door layout, with very few two-door cars built, and the kerb weight was c930kg, which made the Aronde some 30kg heavier than its Czechoslovakian counterpart.

The majority of Arondes had a straight-four 1290cc engine producing 48bhp, which made them marginally more powerful than Octavias, although some Arondes had a smaller 1090cc engine now uprated to 42bhp. Performance of the Aronde and Octavia was largely the same, with the Aronde possibly marginally faster. The most common 1290cc Aronde could achieve 75mph (120km/h), although some sources give 78mph (125km/h) for the very last production cars, and acceleration figures for 0-62mph (0-100km/h) vary from 25 to 30 seconds, again very similar to those for Octavias. The late production Aronde had a slight disadvantage in terms of fuel economy, typically returning c33mpg (8.5l/100km).

Overall, while the Aronde had an edge over the Spartak (see Chapter 2), the Octavia was an equal opponent with some advantages (roadholding, fuel economy, cheaper spare parts) and some disadvantages (only available in two-door form, possibly slightly slower). The Aronde was imported into Czechoslovakia in limited numbers, but I have not found accurate figures. It was sold under the Car Purchase Permit system at prices higher than the Octavia, typically over 40,000 CZK.

The French company gained an advantage with the new Simca Elysée (model P60) launched in late summer 1960. While sharing the engine and slightly tweaked suspension (still with beam-type axle and longitudinal leaf springs in the rear) with its predecessor, this model had a new and completely different four-door body. The P60 was marginally longer and wider but lower than the Aronde, with more interior space. Various engines were available, including the upgraded twin-carburettor 70bhp unit for the sporty Montlhéry model, although the vast majority were the Elysée models with the standard 1290cc 48bhp engine carried over from the Aronde. With its better aerodynamics this model could top 78mph (125km/h) and accelerate from 0 to 62mph (100km/h) in less than 25 seconds. Fuel economy also improved to some 35mpg (8l/100km).

The Elysée competed against the Octavia in European markets including France. Small numbers were imported into Czechoslovakia but, as with the Aronde, accurate figures are not available. I have not succeeded in finding the price, but we can assume that the Elysée was considerably more expensive than the Octavia. It is fair to say that as a family car the Elysée model was superior to any Octavia in most respects. The rare Octavia 1200 TS was quicker than any Elysée other than the limited-production Montlhéry, but still could not match the Simca's space and comfort.

Another French competitor was the Renault Dauphine, a compact four-door car with a small 845cc four-cylinder engine in the rear. The Dauphine was very

*1960 Simca Aronde, restored to very high standard, at a classic car show in my old country. The good looking white-walled tyres were also fitted to some, but not many Octavias in the early 1960s. (Courtesy Zdeněk Patera, www.auta5p.eu).*

*More than a match for the Octavia: Simca Elysée P60 (this car is a 1961 model). (Courtesy Zdeněk Patera, www.auta5p.eu).*

*Renault Dauphine 1960 model: cute and cheeky-looking but losing out against the Octavia on too many counts. (Courtesy Zdeněk Patera, www.auta5p.eu)*

smart-looking with flowing lines, and the 1960-onwards model had power increased to 31 or 32bhp according to various sources. The Dauphine (and its top-of-range Ondine version) was very light: it tipped the scales at 630-650kg depending on the model and equipment, which meant that the small family Renault was not as underpowered as its low power would suggest. Top speed was 72mph (115km/h), similar to the Octavia although the Dauphine had much slower acceleration, taking 37 seconds, or nearly 10 seconds more than its Czechoslovakian counterpart to achieve 62mph (100km/h) from standstill. Fuel economy was excellent, typically 40+mpg (just under 7l/100km).

Regarding the size, the Dauphine was smaller than the Octavia but not by much. It had the advantage of a four-door layout, but was less spacious than the Škoda product and had a much smaller boot. Where the Dauphine fell down was build quality, the very low weight achieved at the expense of sturdiness, and in fact the Dauphine felt rather flimsy. Reliability was not terrible, but not nearly as good as the Octavia. The Dauphine competed against the Octavia in France and other Western European markets, but was not imported into Czechoslovakia.

The French had also come up with the somewhat left-field but technically highly interesting Panhard PL17, a model that was an exact contemporary of the Octavia. Production began in 1959 and ended in 1964, and the Panhard was a quirky car in a very French way. To start with, the designation 17 was an addition of five (CV – fiscal hp in the French tax system), six (for number of passengers) and six (for fuel consumption given at 6l/100km or 46.6mpg). The fuel consumption figure was slightly optimistic, but 40+mpg (just under 7l/100km) was realistic in mixed driving. The PL17 had a small air-cooled flat-twin engine of 851cc capacity typically offering 42bhp, the same as the Octavia with its 1089cc straight-four. There were also more powerful

*The Panhard PL17 was a highly interesting, unconventional design and a tough competitor for any small family car in the early 1960s. High price hampered its sales. (Photograph by Guillaume27, licensed under CC 3.0 via Wikimedia Commons)*

sports versions tuned to 50bhp, but these were quite rare. The Panhard was larger than any other small family car: at 4580mm it was more than 500mm longer than the Octavia and the wheelbase was 2570mm, 180mm longer than the Octavia, while width was 1660mm, again more than the Octavia. As a result, the PL17 was extremely spacious, much more so than the Octavia or Simca Aronde. Indeed, it could (just) accommodate six people including the driver, and although the size of the car could give the impression that it was underpowered, the opposite was true.

The PL17 was very light, its kerb weight of 805kg making it nearly 100kg lighter than the Octavia and some 130kg lighter than the Aronde. This was achieved by extensive use of aluminium in the body. Superb aerodynamics was another feature: I have seen a figure of Cd 0.26! If correct, many modern cars would be put to shame by this more than 60 year-old design. The PL17 was faster than the Octavia (and Simca Aronde), achieving a typical top speed of 82mph (130km/h). Overall, it was a serious competitor for the Octavia, being superior in speed, interior space and fuel economy. The lightweight build resulted in some flimsiness. The Octavia was better built and more durable, possibly with better handling (personal communication from a Panhard owner). However, the main downfall of the PL17 was its price on the French market; significantly higher compared to both the Aronde and Octavia. Unfortunately, I have not found the accurate figure.

In a nutshell, the Octavia was holding its own very well until the end of 1962, mainly because it was a real all-rounder. The strongest points were good interior space for its size, build quality, reliability and longevity. Fuel economy was very good, as were handling and ride. Performance was decent rather than brilliant, with both top speed and acceleration above average for a small family car, but not class-leading. The Octavia's main drawback was the not very practical two-door layout, which inevitably made access to the rear seats more difficult. The small 30-litre petrol tank resulted in a short range of just over 200 miles (320km) with a safe reserve. Finally, and I am sorry to repeat myself, there was the lack of a two-tone paint option. This seemingly minor feature could have made the Octavia even better-looking than it was. In terms of pricing in Western Europe, the Octavia was middle-of-the-range among small family cars.

Car prices generally started coming down in the early 1960s, but none so much as the price of the Octavia. While it cost £745 in 1960 its price was down to £501 by 1964 – almost exactly one third less! Even so, the Octavia was only slightly cheaper than the much more modern Ford Cortina. The reasons for this fall in prices are not entirely clear, but two main explanations spring to mind. Firstly, all cars were becoming cheaper and Škoda had to keep up; secondly, and more importantly, the Octavia's position took a dramatic turn for the worse in late 1962 and, above all in 1963. Two family cars of a new generation made their appearance and rapidly rendered the Octavia severely outdated.

Ford introduced its new small family car, the Cortina 1200 in October 1962 with the straight-four 1198cc 46bhp engine, also fitted to the Anglia 123E. The durability problems plaguing the Anglia 123E were resolved and did not occur in the Cortina, and all versions had a four-speed, fully synchronised gearbox. The new model became available in substantial numbers from early 1963 and swept the competition before it. The more powerful Cortina 1500 with a 1498cc 58bhp engine also joined the range in spring 1963. This model was not a direct competitor to the Octavia, but the smaller-engined Cortina certainly was ... and what a competitor! The monocoque Cortina was more than 200mm longer at 4274mm, and had a 99mm longer wheelbase of 2489mm. While the Cortina's width and height were similar to those of the Octavia, the British car was significantly more spacious and had a larger boot. With 46bhp the Cortina was in fact marginally less powerful than the 1961-on Octavia Super, but it was much lighter. Weighing in at a mere 787kg, the Cortina had a better power-to-weight ratio.

Top speed and acceleration were clearly superior to any Octavia other than a TS or 1200 TS: 80mph (128km/h) and 20 seconds from 0 to 60mph (97km/h) respectively, with 0-62mph (0-100km/h) taking 23 seconds (25.5 seconds according to a different source). In terms of fuel economy, the Cortina was similar to its now obsolete Czechoslovakian counterpart and its ride and handling were very good. Build quality was good and the Cortina soon proved highly reliable. Cortinas were available as two-door or four-door saloons, the latter being the main production model, the estate version joined the range in 1964, and front disc brakes were introduced across the range at the same time. When replaced by the Mk 2 model in late 1966, earlier Cortinas were retrospectively referred to as Mk 1s.

Cortinas were imported into Czechoslovakia from summer 1964 and, interestingly, they were priced quite reasonably (by the standards of 1960s Czechoslovakia) at 48,200 CZK. This made them only slightly more expensive than the Octavia Combi (see Chapter 11) and brand new Škoda 1000 MB (see Chapter 16). The Cortina's superiority to the Octavia was immediately clear, but, more worryingly, the small family Ford was also much superior to the Octavia's successor, the Škoda 1000 MB.

Simca came up with the 1300 in spring 1963. This was a modern small family car very closely comparable to the Cortina, with similar dimensions and general layout. All Simca 1300s were four-door saloons, later joined by a 1500cc model and also an estate version, and the engine was carried over from the older Simca Elysée but upgraded to offer 52bhp from the same 1290cc capacity. At 900kg, the new Simca was of the same weight as the Octavia and heavier than the Cortina.

As it was slightly more powerful than its British counterpart, it had similar

*Mk 1 Ford Cortina 1200: clearly superior to the Octavia in every respect other than similar fuel economy. (Courtesy Zdeněk Patera, www.auta5p.eu).*

*Simca 1300 had a much greater edge over the Octavia than its predecessor the Elysée P60. (Courtesy Zdeněk Patera, www.auta5p.eu).*

performance, top speed given as 80mph (128km/h) or 82mph (130km/h). The 1300 could accelerate from 0 to 62mph (100km/h) in 22.5 seconds. I have not found accurate fuel economy figures, but it can be safely assumed that they were similar to those for the Cortina (and Octavia). Like Cortinas, Simca 1300s were also imported into Czechoslovakia in the mid-1960s and they were mainly available from the Tuzex network (see Chapter 8), priced at 13,200 TK. Small numbers of Simca 1300s were also offered via the state-owned car dealership Mototechna for a crazy 105,000 CZK. Don't ask me why they were more than twice the price of the closely comparable Cortina ...

The appearance of two much more modern competitors at the same time was the end of the road for the good old Octavia. While still a well-built, reliable and economical car, it became totally outdated, and in terms of performance, equipment, space and comfort the Octavia no longer stood a chance against this new generation of cars. The Combi soldiered on until late 1971, but it was fighting a losing battle. It is a matter of deep regret (and an indictment of the directive economy) that the once excellent Octavia was allowed to be outclassed and was not replaced by a successor able to compete with Cortinas and Simcas on equal terms.

CHAPTER 14

# EXOTIC DERIVATIVES

## ŠKODA TREKKA (1966-1973)

**THIS WAS** the first Škoda that would be described as an SUV today. The Trekka was based on the Octavia Combi and built under licence by Motor Industries International Ltd in Otahuhu, New Zealand. A joint effort between Czechoslovakians and New Zealanders, the task was to design a reliable light vehicle for farmers and hunters, substantially smaller and cheaper than a Land Rover.

Mr Josef Velebný of Spartak design fame co-ordinated the work from the Czechoslovakian side, while his New Zealand opposite number was the owner of Motor Industries International Ltd, Mr Noel Turner, assisted by a British designer Mr George Taylor. The contract was signed in late 1965 and the first production Trekka rolled off the production line on 2 December 1966. Interestingly, the plant in Otahuhu did

*Trekka was an Octavia-based SUV built in Otahuhu, New Zealand. (Škoda Museum Storyboard)*

not have sufficient capacity to fully cover the requirements for body panels and some had to be made by a sub-contractor, HJ Ryans, a manufacturer of lawn mowers.

The wheelbase was shortened to 2165mm and ground clearance increased to 190mm, which improved off road manoeuvrability, although the car remained rear-wheel drive. Even so, it had some off-road capability, and in today's terminology it would probably be called a soft-roader. The engine remained the same reliable 1221cc straight-four with 47bhp linked to a four-speed gearbox identical to the Octavia's, and the power was adequate for a small car with a kerb weight of about 950kg. Load carrying capacity was very good at 450kg, 50kg better than for the Octavia Combi, while the Trekka was considerably shorter than the Combi, its length being approximately 3600mm.

The 'soft-roader' was as reliable as the Octavia, and could go to about 69mph (110km/h). Fuel economy remained reasonable at just over 31mpg on average (9l/100km) when driving on the road; when off-roading, the figure dropped to 26-28mpg (10-11l/100km). While the Trekka was never available with four-wheel drive, later cars had a lockable differential as an option, which improved the off-road capability, as did the good ground clearance. The Trekka was available as an estate, pick-up or a beach vehicle, the estate version able to transport up to seven passengers in addition to the driver, six of them sitting on inward-facing benches, Land Rover-style.

Production built up quite quickly with the 1000th Trekka delivered in January 1968 and continued until 1973, some sources indicating the end of production as late 1972 (in *Cars from my Old Country* I previously quoted the end of production as late 1971 but this has turned out to be inaccurate). Trekkas generally performed well and total production was around 2800 cars, or 3000 according to an alternative source. Some were exported to Australia, Indonesia, Samoa, Fiji and even Vietnam, and a few have survived and are now cherished as classics by New Zealand enthusiasts. To my knowledge, one Trekka was even recently imported into the Czech Republic.

## SKOPAK (1967-1971)

SkoPak (an acronym of Škoda and Pakistan) was a car similar to the Trekka but with a longer wheelbase, and was built in Karachi, Pakistan from late 1967. One major difference was the fibreglass body with a fabric roof on most cars, although some SkoPaks were delivered with a fibreglass roof. It had very similar performance, economy and general capability to the Trekka. Unfortunately, production was limited with various sources giving figures of between 1000 and 1400 units, and the 1971 conflict between Eastern Pakistan (now Bangladesh) and Western Pakistan in which India was also involved is given as the main reason for the end of production.

*SkoPak was very similar to the Trekka except for the longer wheelbase and fibreglass body. (Courtesy Zdeněk Patera, www.auta5p.eu)*

CHAPTER 15

# FELICIA TYPE 994 (1959-1964) AND FELICIA SUPER TYPE 996 (1961-1964)

**THE FELICIA** (*Felda* in colloquial Czech) was a 2+2 roadster/hard top coupé derived from the Octavia with which it shared the front part of the body up to the A-pillar. The A-pillar, windscreen and the rest of the body were entirely different. The Felicia was also a logical development of the Škoda 450 (see Chapter 2) but compared to its predecessor, it had a completely different front axle with coil springs, as well as a new rear transverse leaf spring that was the same as the Octavia's. The impact-absorbing steering column was also from the Octavia.

| TABLE 8 | |
|---|---|
| **Škoda Felicia Type 994/Felicia Super Type 996 (1959-1962/1962-1964)** | |
| Length | 4065mm |
| Width | 1600mm |
| Height | 1380mm |
| Wheelbase | 2390mm |
| Kerb weight | 890kg/900kg |
| Bore x stroke | 68x75mm/72x75mm |
| Capacity | 1089cc/1221cc |
| Power | 50bhp/55bhp at 5500/5100rpm |
| Compression ratio | 8.4:1 |
| Top speed | 82mph (130km/h) /85mph (135 km/h)* |
| Acceleration | 0-62mph (0-100km/h) 20/17 seconds |
| Average economy | 31mpg (9l/100km)/ 29.5mpg (9.5l/100km) |
| *Like Octavias, Felicias were slightly faster in real life than the official top speed figures indicate. See page across. | |

The dashboard was of a completely different design, though, usually partly covered in soft black plastic, and the glovebox in front of the passenger was lockable. The speedometer was calibrated up to 160km/h like the TS Octavias, compared to 140km/h in standard models. Early Felicias had the same twin-carburettor 1089cc engine as the Škoda 450, the power of 50bhp adequate for a car marginally lighter than the Octavia, the Felicia tipping the scales at some 890kg. Interestingly, the length and width were the same as the Octavia, even though the Felicia had a largely different body, and the Felicia was also 50mm lower.

The earliest Felicias, built from March 1959, still had a column gear change and bench front seat, but a floor gear change was introduced by early 1960. The Felicia had completely different seats from the Octavia, the separate front items introduced in autumn 1959 being very comfortable, with excellent lateral support by the standards of the time.

The rear seats were relatively cramped, and realistically only suitable for children, although two adults could be transported in the rear for short distances and with limited comfort. Interestingly, the boot had the same 300-litre capacity as the Octavia, which made the Felicia a good car for a long weekend away ... but very few people

*Early (probably autumn 1959) Felicia with column gear change, no fins on rear wings but separate front seats. The very smart black paint was less common than bright red. All early Felicias had a 1089cc engine.*

could afford long weekends away in 1960s Czechoslovakia!

Performance was identical to the Octavia TS and 1200 TS (see Chapter 9) even though the Felicia was a little lighter. This made the 1221cc Felicia Super, the main production model from early 1962, a credible sports car. Like Octavias, Felicias slightly exceeded the official top speed figures in real life, and a well-maintained Super could briefly touch 88mph (140km/h), while those with the smaller 1089cc engine could achieve nearly 85mph (135km/h), again provided they were in good condition. Ride and handling were similar to the Octavia, although the Felicia felt generally more agile, and fuel economy was also the same as in 'hot' Octavias. We can only speculate on how a more powerful engine, possibly around 1600cc, would have further improved performance and handling. Such an engine would probably have put the Felicia on a par with superb British convertibles such as the Triumph Vitesse or Sunbeam Alpine.

All Felicias were convertibles with a good quality fabric roof, but an interchangeable fibreglass hardtop became available in spring 1960. The hardtops were often in an ivory colour, very smart in combination with the typically red or less common black body. A slightly longer hard top of new design was introduced in 1961.

As with the Octavia, fins on the rear wings were introduced from January 1961. Build quality was very good, the Felicia just as reliable and long-lasting as the Octavia, and maintenance was generally straightforward, but correct setting of the twin carburettors required some experience. The Felicia was successfully exported to many European countries and became a good source of the hard currency the regime was desperate for. Some two thirds of the 14,863 Felicias built in total were exported, mostly to Western Europe but, even so, the Felicia was always

*Late production Felicia Super with a 1221cc engine. These were identified by small 'Super' inscriptions under the decorative side skirts on the front wings and on the rear just below the boot lid. Note the aftermarket period wheel trims often fitted to export models. The external mirrors became standard on Felicias (but not Octavias) in 1963.*

disliked and seen as 'decadent' by the upper echelons of the Communist Party. The price on the domestic market was set arbitrarily and quite high at 42,000 CZK in 1960. By 1964, it was 46,400 CZK (c31 average monthly salaries) including the hardtop.

Felicias were built exclusively in the Kvasiny plant, and although the proportion of Supers is not clear one source gives a figure of 3201 cars. However, this is not entirely reliable as some were probably built in 1961, before they became the main production model. Production of all Felicias was much slower from 1962 onwards, because the Octavia Combi, also built in Kvasiny, had priority. The last Felicia Super rolled off the assembly line in late June 1964, just over two months after production of the Octavia had ended in the main plant in Mladá Boleslav.

The Felicia has a permanent place in the hearts of Czech and Slovak classic car enthusiasts, even though only about 5000 remained in Czechoslovakia. Spare parts supply is very good.

## HOW DID THE FELICIA COMPARE?

The Felicia was always a niche product, a car built in relatively small numbers and aimed at a limited circle of potential customers. There was no similar car built in the Eastern Bloc, therefore the Felicia competed only against small Western European cars with a sporty

While I was never a Felicia driver, I cannot fail to share this memory. When I was a young man in the late 1970s and early 1980s, my idea of a great day out was driving a Felicia, ideally a bright red Super, with the hood down and wind in my hair, through the lovely Czech countryside on a sunny day, and with a beautiful young lady sitting next to me. Well ... dream on, Mirek! Obviously, I could not afford a Felicia.

Given the current prices I will never be able to afford it, but I honestly don't mind. I have done way better: I have found my lovely lady. I first met Markéta in a rather interesting way, probably unheard of in Europe. We met at a political meeting organised by the Socialist Union of Youth (youth organisation of the Communist Party). Neither of us wanted to attend that meeting, but attendance was expected and we had good reasons to comply. I was no longer a supporter of Communism by then, but I had been as a teenager when I believed that Communism was all about fairness and equal opportunities. Yes, I realise now that it was a strikingly absurd view, and in fact quite rare among young Czechs and Slovaks in the mid-1970s.

Like almost all similarly misguided youngsters, I 'grew out' of my Communist sympathies by my early twenties. However, I was in my final year at the Medical School and looking for a job. Falling out with the Communist Party was not a bright idea as the party branches at the workplace had a major say in who would get a job. Therefore, I made a rather late decision to attend that meeting even though I had a few days off after passing some important exams. Prior to my departure for the meeting, I had been making a model of the Spitfire (my favourite old aeroplane ... yes, it was OK to be a Spitfire enthusiast at this late stage of Communism). I was very shabbily dressed in my oldest jeans and a jumper that had seen better days, so I had no qualms about wiping glue off my fingers on that jumper! I did not have enough time to get changed, let alone to shave, so I came to the meeting looking rather scruffy ... and regretted it the moment I saw Markéta.

She was just over half way through her university course and attended the meeting for a similar reason as me. She clearly did not want to be there; her expression was sad, bored and unhappy. Even so, I thought she was stunningly beautiful in a kind, intelligent way. Being immediately impressed by Markéta, I made sure I was sitting next to her. The meeting was as boring and pointless as expected, but I instantly forgot about falling asleep. This was what many people did at such meetings, and they usually got away with it by the early 1980s. In fact, I had fallen asleep at a similar meeting some months before only to be asked how many students from my year had attended the 'May Day Rally of The Working People'! I woke up and said the first figure that somehow came to my mind: "One hundred and twenty-eight". The figure bore not the slightest resemblance to reality, but I was praised as there were one hundred and forty students in my year.

This meeting was very different: My heart was leaping when I started talking to Markéta quietly and tried to cheer her up. To my delight, she brightened up and smiled, which made her even more beautiful. So, I took my chances, asked her for a date and was amazed that she agreed. When we met for that date a few days later, I was very smartly turned out ... and Markéta took a few seconds to recognise me as she was looking out for that shabby character from the meeting!

We have now been married for 40 years, but I have never taken my lady for a day out in (ideally) a bright red Felicia Super ... what a failure. Sorry, Markéta!

*Triumph Herald 13/60 Convertible was a tough competitor for any Felicia. (Courtesy Zdeněk Patera, www.auta5p.eu)*

character (rather than out-and-out sports cars). That category was not particularly crowded even in Western Europe.

The most obvious British competitor was the Triumph Herald Coupé or Convertible, the former strictly a two-seater, the latter a 2+2 like the Felicia. Early cars had the 34bhp 948cc engine fitted with twin carburettors, which compensated for its lack of power to some extent, but even so these models would be at a disadvantage against the Felicia (let alone Felicia Super) in terms of performance. Once the 1147cc engine was fitted from spring 1961 onwards, the performance was close to that of the Felicia, and the Herald was always more manoeuvrable.

The Herald 12/50 available as a Convertible (not Coupé) from mid-1963 offered 51bhp and its top speed and acceleration were similar to the figures for the 1089cc Felicia at 82mph (130km/h) and a 0-60mph (0-97km/h) time of 21.5 seconds. The Herald 13/60 introduced in August 1967 had 61bhp to play with and could turn the tables on any Felicia, and like the 12/50, it was available as a Saloon, Estate and Convertible. Its official top speed was 85mph (135km/h), but it could briefly go to 88mph (140km/h) in real life, making the 13/60 as fast as the Felicia Super, while its acceleration was probably slightly better. Even the 13/60 Convertible, while heavier than earlier Heralds, was still significantly lighter than the Felicia at 838kg versus 890kg, which gave the late production Herald a better power-to-weight ratio.

While the Felicia was a smart-looking car, some might find the Giovanni Michelotti-penned Herald Coupé or Convertible more elegant. The laminated wood dashboards of later sporty Heralds were an additional attractive feature. Overall, it is probably fair to say that the sporty Heralds were evenly matched with Felicias (including the fuel economy), rather like saloon models with Octavias.

*Much cooler than the Felicia: the VW Karmann Ghia Convertible, a late 1500 model from 1970. (Courtesy Zdeněk Patera, www.auta5p.eu )*

Germany (then West Germany) also had a car in this category: the VW Karmann Ghia or Type 14. This was a world-beating combination of German build quality and Italian design, albeit with modest mechanicals based on the VW Beetle. Later models also shared some mechanicals with the Volkswagen Type 3 Variant. Discussions started as early as 1952 between Wilhelm Karmann, the owner of Karmann coachbuilders, and Luigi Segre the head of Carozzeria Ghia about creating a small, stylish and moderately practical 2+2 convertible and coupé, but not a real sports car, based on the widely available (and by then well-tried) VW Beetle.

When they agreed on the basic design, Karmann secured the support of VW. He was already well-connected there, as his company had been building the Beetle Convertible, while other great Italian designers such as Mario Boano, Sergio Coggiola and Giovanni Savonuzzi of the Ghia team were also involved in the original design. There are claims that many ideas from the contemporary designs of the famous Virgil Exner were incorporated with his consent. In fact, Segre and Exner were close professionally and personally, and Segre arranged for the very first Karmann Ghia exported to the US to be donated to Exner. VW approved the design in November 1953 and preparations for production started.

The first Karmann Ghia coupés rolled off the production line in August 1955, joined by the convertible in August 1957. The early models had a somewhat weedy air-cooled 1192cc 34bhp flat-four shared with contemporary Beetles, although an alternative source gives the power as 36bhp. Thanks to much better aerodynamics, they could just top 75mph (120km/h). The 1300 model with a 1285cc 39bhp engine was introduced in 1963, and its top speed was 80mph (128km/h); I could not find the acceleration figure for the 1200 model, but the 1300's 0-62mph (0-100km/h) time was 27 seconds. All Karmann Ghias were comparatively light, with a typical kerb weight around 830kg, and the performance received a major boost with the introduction of the 1493cc engine in 1967. This offered 49bhp, with top speed increased to 85mph (135km/h) and I found a 0-62mph (0-100km/h) acceleration figure of 23 seconds.

The ultimate Karmann Ghia was launched in 1970, with power increased to 60bhp from its 1584cc engine. This model could achieve 91mph (145km/h) and the acceleration was also significantly better at c18 seconds for the 0-62mph (0-100km/h) sprint. However, these cars were never about speed and acceleration; they were very good-looking, relaxed boulevard cruisers, and all versions were highly reliable and reasonably economical at 31mpg (c9l/100 km) on average.

The total production was 445,238 cars built between 1955 and 1974, this number almost 30 times(!) that of the Felicia. The majority were coupés (364,401 units) and in addition 41,689 (again mostly coupés) were built in Brazil between 1962 and 1975.

So how did the Felicia compare with its German counterpart? The two cars were evenly matched in terms of reliability and economy and the Felicia had a performance advantage over the 1200 and 1300 models, but lost it when up against the 1500s and, particularly, 1600s. More importantly, it came nowhere near the production figures, nor the brilliant exterior design of the Karmann Ghia. On the latter count, the Felicia lost against one of the coolest cars of all time.

France had a moderately sporty 2+2 model also based on a small family car, this being the Renault Floride/Caravelle derived from the popular Dauphine. Renault management were envious of the VW Karmann Ghia's commercial success, particularly in the US, and wanted to offer a comparable car. The American Renault dealers were also asking for a small 2+2 able to compete with the Karmann Ghia. The crucial meeting took place in Florida, therefore the car was originally referred to as the Floride, but it was soon recognised that the name might not be suitable in other US states and the name Caravelle was adopted. The Floride name was only used on the European market until March 1962 when it was also changed to Caravelle.

Design work started in 1956 with Pietro Frua of Carrozzeria Ghia responsible for designing the body. He did a good job, particularly given the limitations of the Dauphine floor pan and engine, and the result was a good-looking 2+2, 320mm longer than the Dauphine with quite noticeable overhangs at the front and rear. The new Renault was launched at the 1958 Paris Motor Show, with the 845cc engine as fitted to the Dauphine but tuned to offer 37bhp. When sales started in the early summer of 1959, the Gordini version with 40bhp was also available. The engine was in the rear, but in contrast to the VW it was liquid-cooled and, unlike the Felicia, Triumph Herald and VW, the Floride initially had a three-speed gearbox with synchromesh on the top two gears. This early model was somewhat underpowered, only achieving 76mph (122km/h) but I have not found any acceleration figures.

The updated model, now called the Caravelle, was launched in March 1962. The bodywork was more aerodynamically refined, but the main difference was a more powerful 956cc 48bhp engine, which increased top speed to 82mph (130km/h). Another major advantage of this model was disc brakes on all wheels, an advanced feature in the early 1960s. The early Caravelle only remained in production until mid-1964, when a new 1108cc 55bhp engine became available, this final model offering much improved performance. When tested by the British *Autocar* magazine in November 1965, the updated Caravelle achieved a top speed of 89mph (just under 143km/h) and accelerated from 0-60mph (0-97km/h) in 17.8 seconds. Fuel economy was recorded as 30.2mpg (9.4l/100km) in mixed

*Late production Renault Caravelle with the more powerful 1108cc engine was evenly matched with the Felicia Super. (Courtesy Zdeněk Patera, www.auta5p.eu).*

driving, similar to the competitors. This model remained in production until 1968 and the total production run was just over 117,000. Approximately two-thirds were Caravelles. As with the VW Karmann Ghia, the early models were less powerful and slower than the Felicia, but with the arrival of the Caravelle in 1964 the Felicia lost its performance advantage.

The styling of the Caravelle is open to debate; in my personal view, the French car was not as good-looking as its VW competitor, but possibly more stylish than the Felicia.

In summary, the Felicia was initially holding its own well, and indeed had a performance edge over the early models of its competitors. Other plus points were its build quality and reliability, but, unfortunately, it was not developed further, and gradually became unable to keep up with modernised European cars of its class. The slow production of Felicias was another disadvantage, the total production run from 1959 to 1964 being less than 15,000 cars, a small fraction of the figures for comparable European cars.

Even the relatively rare Triumph Herald Coupé and Convertible models were built in several times higher numbers (combined production of both versions was 87,496 cars). Had the Felicia been continuously developed and built in much higher numbers, it could have been a real contender, although never as stylish as the VW Karmann Ghia. Instead, it became yet another example of a quality product being held back by the limits of the directive economy.

CHAPTER 16

# THE CAR THAT REPLACED THE OCTAVIA

## ŠKODA 1000 MB/1100 MB TYPE 721 (1964-1969)

**THE ŠKODA** 1000 MB (*Embéčko* in colloquial Czech) represented a radical departure from the then current Škoda design. The MB stood for Mladá Boleslav where the cars were made, and first studies into the new design started in the late 1950s when the Spartak (see Chapter 2) was still rolling off the production lines. The task was to design a small family car that was affordable to wide sections of the population, had a kerb weight of 700kg and fuel economy of 40mpg (7l/100km) as specified by the Communist Party and Government. It was planned to increase production significantly in comparison with the Spartak and even the Octavia. Substantial funds were released by the authorities and invested into a major extension of the main Škoda factory in Mladá Boleslav; new halls were built and new assembly lines installed.

Several prototypes of various layouts were built, and a decision was made early on to abandon the traditional front engine and rear-wheel drive layout because it was considered too heavy and also expensive to manufacture. One of the prototypes tested a front-wheel drive arrangement, but finally it was decided to focus on the 'all in the rear' layout, some inspiration coming from the (by then outdated) VW Beetle and successful Renault designs, the Dauphine and 8. Production expenses were also considered to be lower with such a layout. However, this layout was becoming less popular by the early 1960s, the main reason being that such a design made it extremely difficult to derive estate or commercial versions from the basic model. Further prototypes were successfully tested and they bore an increasing resemblance to the production Škoda 1000 MB as it emerged in April 1964.

The new model was totally unrelated to its predecessor, the Octavia. It was a rear-engine car of unitary construction, the latter used for the first time in a Škoda, and with the exception of the sporty MBX version, all 1000 MBs were four-door saloons, which made access to the rear seats much easier. The new engine was liquid-cooled like that of the Octavia, but smaller and lighter: a four-cylinder OHV of 988cc capacity weighing 83kg (Octavia engine weighed around 100kg). It had an aluminium cylinder block which was an advanced feature in 1964, it was a square engine with the same 68mm bore and stroke, and power was 42bhp, like the Octavia. Torque was also very similar, initially 68.5Nm, then from 1966 onwards 73.5Nm. The engine was relatively high-revving, achieving its maximum power output at 4650rpm.

The 1000 MB was significantly lighter that the Octavia, and, while it was not possible to achieve the originally specified kerb weight of 700kg, it weighed in at just under 800kg. Screw-and-nut steering and hydraulic drum brakes were fitted, and suspension was all-independent in Škoda tradition, but coil springs were now fitted front and rear. The four-speed gearbox

*Early Škoda 1000 MB. Note the shape of the louvres on the rear wing, typical of 1964-1966 models.*

*Late production Škoda 1000 MB, 1968-on. Note the simplified straight louvres on the rear wing and thicker C-pillar.*

*Škoda 1000/1100 MBX was smart-looking, but not sufficiently powerful to make a convincing sports car. Small numbers were built and they are now very rare.*

was fully synchronised. The 1000 MB was 4170mm long, 1620mm wide, and 1390mm high, and interior space was adequate to carry four passengers in reasonable comfort, although five passengers could be carried over short distances. The boot in front was relatively small, but there was another luggage compartment behind the rear seats and the total luggage capacity was actually bigger than in the Octavia, at 340 vs 300 litres.

The increase in performance compared to the Octavia was modest, the 1000 MB able to go to 75mph (120km/h), with cars built from 1966 marginally faster, achieving 78mph (125km/h). The 0-62mph (100km/h) time was typically 27 seconds, again not much different from the Octavia, and the new Škoda was economical, returning 35-40mpg (7-8l/100km). As expected with the rear-engine layout, the 1000 MB had a tendency to oversteer, but overall handling was reasonable. Prices were still high: earliest cars cost 44,000 CZK, the 1965 model with slightly improved equipment came to 45,600 CZK, which was an equivalent of about 30 average monthly salaries.

Production was increasing fast and new versions were gradually introduced. The second most-produced model, albeit built in relatively limited numbers, was the 1000 MB de Luxe, with a better equipped interior. The 1000 MBG with twin-carburettor 988cc engine came in 1966, with power increased to 52bhp and a top speed of just over 80mph (128km/h) with a 0-62mph (0-100km/h) time of about 23 seconds. The 1000 MBX also joined the range in mid-1966. This was a two-door saloon with the same engine and identical performance. Some later cars had a slightly larger twin-carburettor 1107cc engine, but performance gains were small. Both sporty versions were still reasonably economical, returning nearly 35mpg (just over 8l/100km). Prices were around 52,000 CZK, significantly higher compared to standard cars.

A more powerful version, the 1100 MB, using the 1107cc engine in single-carburettor guise, was introduced in late 1967. The differences from the 988cc engine were the bore increased to 72mm and power was 48bhp. The 1100 MB was marginally faster than the 1000 MB, and could accelerate better with the 0-62mph (0-100km/h) sprint taking some 23 seconds.

The last facelift to the range came in the summer of 1968 with the wider C-pillar and slightly different front valance. Some of these cars were delivered as 1000 or 1100 MB de Luxe with minor improvements to the interior, and they sold for about 49,000 CZK.

Production ended in the autumn of 1969 when the new 100/110 model was phased in. Overall, the 1000 MB range was quite successful, and, while these early rear-engined Škodas were not quite as solid as Octavias, build quality was decent. Teething troubles were soon ironed out and reliability was good, and significant numbers of 1000 MBs and 1100 MBs were exported. However, the 1000 MB was always at some disadvantage against the Ford Cortina Mk 1 and Simca 1300, and with the arrival of the updated Ford Cortina Mk 2 (in 1300 guise) and Simca 1301 in 1966, the 1000 MB's position became weaker still. Even the 1967 1100 MB was not the answer.

Not only was it still inferior to its main competitors, but it was also built in inadequate numbers (see below). Substantial numbers of survivors are now cherished as classics in both the Czech and Slovak Republics.

Production figures are given below:

| | |
|---|---|
| 1000 MB (the main production model) | 349,348 |
| 1000 MB de Luxe | 65,502 |
| 1000 MBG | 3287 |
| 1000 MBX | 1403 |
| 1100 MB | 22,487 |
| 1100 MBX | 1114 |
| **Total:** | **443,141** |

CHAPTER 17

# THE CAR THAT *SHOULD* HAVE REPLACED THE OCTAVIA

## ŠKODA TYPE 720 (1967-1971)

**THE ADVANCED** 720 is a very Czechoslovakian 'could have been'. It was soon recognised that the 1000 MB and 1100 MB, while performing fairly well, could not compete on equal terms with modern European small family cars such as the Ford Cortina Mk 2 or Simca 1301/1501. A larger, more powerful car was needed, and the Škoda design team started work in mid-1967. In fact, there had been preliminary studies since the early 1960s, but the authorities decided to give priority to the 1000 MB. Interestingly, the early studies included a small, straight-six 1482cc, 65bhp engine! The new Škoda was gradually taking shape from early 1967 and the design was finalised by mid-1968.

The main asset was the completely new light alloy straight-four OHC engine, a first for a Škoda. The engine was designed in such a way that the capacity could be easily increased; this was referred to as assembly kit design. The main technical data of the 720 is given in Table 9.

The figures relate to later, Giugiaro-bodied prototypes. The smaller engine was significantly oversquare, which made it quite high-revving, and torque was a decent 98Nm, while the 1498cc engine had 125Nm. Both engines were built, successfully tested and fitted to prototypes. All 720 engines had Jikov or Weber carburettors, single in saloons and estates, twin in sports models, and, unlike previous Škodas, the 720 was fitted with an alternator from the start.

TABLE 9

| Škoda 1250/1500 Type 720 (1967-1972) | |
|---|---|
| Length | 4373mm |
| Width | 1653mm |
| Height | 1465mm |
| Wheelbase | 2550mm |
| Kerb weight | 1000kg/1030kg |
| Bore x stroke | 80x61.5mm/80x74.5mm |
| Capacity | 1236cc/1498cc |
| Power | 67bhp*/84*bhp at 5700/5300rpm |
| Compression ratio | Not found |
| Top speed | 88mph (140km/h)/97mph (155km/h) ** |
| Acceleration | 0-62mph (0-100km/h) 22.5***/18.8 seconds |
| Average economy | 31mpg (9l/100km)/29.5mpg (9.5l/100km) |

**Alternative sources give figures of 70 and 85bhp respectively.*
***Alternative sources give top speed of the 1500 model as 99mph (158km/h)*
****Alternative figure of 24.2 seconds for the 1250 model is also given*

At least one 1771cc engine (or 1772cc according to an alternative source) intended for a sports version and possibly some estates

*First estate prototype built in Vrchlabí, seen here probably in November 1968, before Italdesign became involved. (Courtesy Škoda archive, Mladá Boleslav, Czech Republic)*

was built, run on a test bed and probably fitted to a fastback prototype. This engine offered 95bhp at 5200rpm with 152Nm torque. The biggest 1997cc engine was designed but, to the best of my knowledge, not built. All the engines had crankshafts with five main bearings, a major improvement on earlier three-bearing engines.

Gearboxes initially fitted to the prototypes had four speeds with full synchromesh. Traditionally for a Škoda, the 720 had independent suspension in the front and rear; front axle was of MacPherson type with torsion bar stabilisers, and there were semi-trailing arms at the rear. Disc brakes in front were another first in a Škoda, and the only outdated feature was the screw-and-nut steering, but it was expected to be replaced with rack-and-pinion in production cars.

The building of prototypes started in late 1967, but the progress accelerated considerably in 1968, with the first saloon prototype tested on 12 August. This was soon followed by the first estate prototype. The first prototype with the Guigiaro-designed body was a 1500 saloon model completed on 30 August 1969, just over a year after the Soviet occupation.

The 720 was of unitary construction, but difficulties were encountered when designing the body; in particular, torsional stiffness was not sufficient. Eventually, Škoda approached various Italian design teams and an agreement was reached with Giorgetto Giugiaro of Italdesign in early 1969. The Italians designed elegant bodies for four-door saloon and estate versions, as well as a two-door fastback, making the 720 a modern small to medium-size family car. Compared to the Ford Cortina Mk 3 it was marginally longer but narrower. Further prototypes were built, their total number probably reaching 15; the majority were four-door saloons, but there were also estates, sporty two-door fastbacks/hatchbacks and coupés.

Both main versions performed well as shown in Table 9. The Škoda 1250, as the smaller-engined car was referred to, was obviously slower but more economical. The fastback was the only 720 model just topping 100mph (161km/h) and according to one source this prototype, tested from July 1971, had the larger 1771cc engine. Interestingly, there was also one fastback prototype with the entry-level 1236cc engine, but it was underpowered for a sports car. An estate

*Škoda 720-1250 with a Giugiaro-designed body, probably autumn 1969 or spring 1970. Single headlights were typical of the entry-level model. Does this Škoda look a little like the later Fiat 132, or is it just in my head?*

prototype with a 1498cc engine had been completed shortly before, in June 1971. More estate prototypes followed and extensively tested, one of them covering 45,000km (28,000 miles) with no problems and, in fact, one 1500 saloon covered as much as 80,000km (50,000 miles), also entirely trouble-free. The plan was to fit all estate models with larger engines of at least 1498cc, but also of 1771cc capacity.

All 720s had very good handling and a comfortable ride, and their performance and economy were comparable to those of contemporary European cars of the same class. Teething troubles were neither numerous nor major. Further improvements, such as air-conditioning, rack-and-pinion steering, servo-assisted disc brakes all round and a five-speed gearbox were planned and designed for production cars, initially for those at the higher end of the range. Sporting models with the 1771cc engines were to have Laycock overdrives imported from the UK, until a Czechoslovakian-made five-speed gearbox would become available. According to some sources, one Laycock overdrive was actually tested in a fastback prototype, and even ABS, air suspension, fuel injection and a three-speed automatic gearbox were under consideration as possible future options.

The original plan was to start production in 1970, build 100,000 cars per year by 1973, and increase production above 120,000 cars by 1975. This would have been more than the annual production of the Octavia, or indeed 1000 MB. However, progress was much slower after the Soviet occupation, and production was due to start in early 1973 with saloons built in the main Mladá Boleslav plant while estates were to be built in Vrchlabí. Sporty fastback (and possibly hatchback) models from the Kvasiny plant were to join the range in 1974.

I have found prices suggested for the 720 saloons. The 720-1250 (entry level) was to cost 30,000 CZK, while the 1500 model would have been 35,000 CZK. How realistic these proposals were is open to discussion, particularly because they were considerably lower than prices of the smaller 1000/1100

*Škoda 720-1500, original picture probably from 1970-71. Note the twin headlights, different radiator grille, decorative wheel caps and sideskirts.*

MB. I have not found any prices proposed for the estate or fastback models.

Had it gone into production, the Škoda 720 would, most likely, have been highly successful on both domestic and export markets, even if the prices were higher than those given above. Good build quality and reliability could be realistically expected. The 720 fitted with larger engines (1.5-litre and above) would have compared favourably not only with volume-manufactured compact family cars like the Ford Cortina Mk 3, Fiat 131 Mirafiori or French Simca-Chrysler 160/180, but could even have competed with the BMW 1600 series.

So why did this promising design not reach production? The reasons were some 90 per cent political and 10 percent economic. Let us cover the economic aspects first. The 720 was completely unrelated to the rear-engined 1000/1100 MB, so new machinery and assembly lines would have to be installed. This would have been expensive. In the state-controlled, directive economy of Czechoslovakia funding was totally dependent on political support or, to call a spade a spade, on the whims of the highest-ranking members of the Central Committee of the Communist Party. The timing could hardly have been worse: the attempt at reforming Communism was crushed by Soviet tanks rolling into Czechoslovakia in the early hours of 21 August 1968.

The occupation of Czechoslovakia, the second in less than 30 years, ended what pro-Soviet Communists called 'The period of crisis'. It is beyond the scope of this book to cover all aspects of the Soviet occupation, but suffice to say that moderate, reformist Communists, but also highly qualified non-party members, were systematically removed from leading positions and replaced by those who unreservedly supported the 'Entry of Warsaw Pact forces' (while some 90% of the occupation forces were Soviet there were token units from other Warsaw Pact armies also involved).

The 'Normalisation' as referred to by the pro-Soviet Communists was begun. Investigation Committees (see Chapter 1) were set up all over the country to scrutinise

*This not very clear picture shows the dashboard of the Škoda 720-1500 saloon. The design is very 1970s, complete with wood veneer. (Courtesy Škoda archive, Mladá Boleslav, Czech Republic).*

every employee for loyalty to the Communist Party and Soviet Union, and people were invited to attend an interview before the Committee and asked about their political views. The Committee had also obtained references from 'reliable Comrades' prior to the interview, which opened the way for abuse of power, corruption and settling scores. Stakes were extremely high as careers and livelihoods were under threat, and indeed, many people lost their jobs and became second class citizens for decades to come. Anyone found to disagree with the occupation – sorry ... 'Entry of Warsaw Pact forces'– was sacked. New legislation making it possible to sack anyone for disagreeing with any aspect of the Communist Party policies was introduced in a hurry. The purges peaked in 1969-1970, but continued until late 1971, and after that, people were still sacked on an individual basis but no longer in huge numbers.

There was a popular story circulating in Czechoslovakia in the 1970s and 1980s suggesting that the Soviets had asked the Czechoslovakian Comrades to cancel the 720 project in order to remove superior competition for their Lada cars. I had long believed this story, but after more thorough research I have to admit to my mistake. While it is true that the 720 would have been vastly superior to any Lada model, including the heavily modified versions from the late 1970s and even early 1980s, there is no evidence of Soviet interference. There are no documents or witness statements to that effect, and, in fact, production of Ladas was barely adequate and the cars were exported at the expense of the Soviet domestic market.

Like the Czechoslovakians, the Soviets were also aiming to increase private car ownership at that time, which makes it highly unlikely that they would have minded the Czechoslovakians designing and making their own cars. While it was popular (and understandable) to blame the Soviets for almost everything after the 1968 occupation, they were not guilty in this case. The indigenous Comrades were entirely responsible for killing off the superb 720, which to my mind makes the story particularly sad.

The Škoda company (then officially called AZNP) was hit very hard by the purges. Indeed, it was very nearly put out of business. Could it have been the revenge for 1958 (see Chapter 2)? Many highly qualified, motivated designers, engineers and skilled workers were sacked and replaced by often utterly incompetent individuals, but that should not come as a surprise. The regime always valued unreserved loyalty to the Communist Party and its policies (whatever they were) more than knowledge, skills and human qualities, and highly competent professionals were often seen as a potential problem. The purges were followed by the long decline in both the design and build quality of Škodas, which started in the early 1970s and lasted until the late 1980s when the Favorit came along against the odds. The decline is best exemplified by the sad Škoda 120, known as the Estelle in the UK and the even worse (yes, you can always set a new standard!) Škoda 105.

Some able people survived, and even continued developmental work on the 720 and other projects. Prototypes were successfully tested until early 1972, with calculated performance and economy figures mostly confirmed, but the whole development was watched by the 'purified' Communist Party with increasing hostility. The Škoda 720 was a product of 'The period of crisis' and, as such had to be abolished, destroyed, trampled into the ground! In particular, the involvement of Italdesign made the pro-Soviet Communists livid. The undisputable qualities of the well-designed new Škoda cut no ice with them, and indeed seemed to have merely increased their hatred.

The inevitable happened on 18 April 1971. The Communist Party instigated a directive from the Ministry of Industry to transfer production to Bratislava Automobile Works (BAZ or Bratislavské Automobilové Závody in Slovak) in the Slovak capital, Bratislava. This was cunning: no such factory existed. In 1971 there was only a small, if highly capable design office in Bratislava with a prototype workshop but little machinery and no production lines. The Communist Party was fully aware of this and deliberately ordered transfer of production to a non-existent factory! Remarkably, according to some sources the Slovaks built two further 1500 prototypes (one saloon and one estate) in the prototype workshop, but there were no facilities for mass production. Construction of the BAZ factory only started in late 1974, and limited production of an unrelated model started there in 1981; that was the rear-engined Škoda Garde 2+2 sports car based on the 120 Series (Estelle in the UK).

Interestingly, the decision made in April 1971 was only announced to the public in late 1972. Just to be on the safe side, the Ministry of Industry officially terminated work on the Škoda 720 project in November 1972. Why the Communist Party decided to kill off the 720 in this way rather than merely banning production is a matter of speculation. There are various explanations ranging from logical to absurd, as many Czechs (and Slovaks) are given to conspiracy theories, but I am inclined to believe that there was a secondary motive: apart from killing off the new Škoda it was also aiming to drive a wedge between Czechs and Slovaks by frustrating both. The relationship between the two nations has always been good (football and ice hockey rivalries aside!), so it is conceivable that high-ranking Comrades of both nationalities were worried about Czechs and Slovaks jointly deciding that they have had enough of the Communist Party ...

The purges that nearly destroyed Škoda were replicated in all companies and offices up and down my old country, usually with similarly devastating results. It is probably fair to say that the economic, social and moral damage lasted for decades, possibly with some after-effects persisting even today. I cannot help adding my personal memory of how I saw that time as a very young adolescent. Hopefully, this digression will be of some help in understanding the sheer absurdity of the social climate in Czechoslovakia in the late 1960s and early 1970s.

I was a teenager in the making at the time and, after more than half a century I still remember very well how worried my parents were that they would lose their jobs. I was frightened and confused as I could not work out why my parents or anyone else should lose the job they were doing well just because of their views. Rather ironically, while I did not agree with the purges and the presence of Soviet forces in Czechoslovakia, I became a (temporary) supporter of Communism in my late teens. That is a very Czechoslovakian example of absurdity!

My parents retained their jobs even though they disagreed with the Soviet occupation. My dad was at particularly high risk: his negative view of the occupation was well known. Thankfully, the system was less than perfect. As a result, my dad had an extremely close shave. He worked for a state-owned commercial company that was dealt with by a particularly thorough Investigation Committee.

The Committee was led by an extreme Communist, a real ideological maniac sacking people left, right and centre. He was fully aware of the consequences for those affected, but had no problem with gleefully destroying people's livelihoods and taking away their children's futures in the name of an absurd ideological principle. This man was also an alcoholic. He ended up in hospital with multiple drink-related problems and never came out. This happened only days before he would have interviewed, and almost certainly sacked, my dad.

His replacement was a completely decent, sensible man strikingly different to most other Communists in his position. He must have been appointed by some mistake. Like my dad, this new Chairman was a member of the hunting community, so my dad's interview was focussed on hunting game! According to family recollections, the new Chairman started the interview by asking: "Comrade Synek, how would you describe the significance of the Warsaw Pact armies' entry?" My dad said gravely: "It has certainly saved Socialism* in Czechoslovakia." "Quite so" replied the chairman in an equally serious voice and then changed the subject: "I hear you are a fellow hunter." "That's right" confirmed my dad and the conversation took a much safer direction! Thankfully, the other members of the Committee were there just to make up the numbers and did not dare to intervene. Amazingly, no other 'reliable Comrade' attempted to create problems for my dad and he was allowed to retain his job.

Just for good measure, no one else from the company was sacked from then on. The newly appointed Chairman reported that his predecessor had done such an excellent job that there were no 'counter-revolutionaries' left for him to sack! My dad and many other people did not lose their livelihoods through pure chance, simply because one lunatic had drunk himself to death and then some senior Communist official made a mistake of appointing a gentleman as his replacement.

*Oddly enough, the leading Communists referred to their regime as Socialism or Real Socialism while maintaining that they (and 'The Working People') were building Communism.

*Škoda 720 fastback as tested in early 1971. The 1771cc engine was to be the main power unit for this model, although lower-powered versions were also considered. Note the wheels similar to British Rostyles from the 1970s. (Courtesy Škoda archive, Mladá Boleslav, Czech Republic)*

*Guigiaro-designed Škoda 720 estate with a 1.5- or 1.8-litre engine would have been a very elegant yet spacious estate, competitive with its European counterparts. (Courtesy www.auto.cz)*

*Škoda 720-1500 saloon, one of the surviving prototypes. This would have been the main production model and the cars would have looked very much like this. (Courtesy Škoda archive/skoda-team.cz, Mladá Boleslav, Czech Republic).*

On a more positive note, I recall seeing one 720 saloon parked in Prague, probably in autumn 1971. As a young teenager very much into cars and aeroplanes, I was seriously impressed by its design and build quality and, better still, several Škoda 720s have survived to this day. One 1250 saloon can be admired in the Škoda Museum in Mladá Boleslav but I am not clear whether it is exhibited at present. At least one 1500 saloon is said to be registered to a private owner in Prague, and one more in the town of Krupina, Slovakia. I have learned that there is now a 720 estate exhibited at the new museum Svět Škodovek (Czech for The World of Škodas), just opened near the town of Benešov some 35 miles (56km) south-east of Prague. One fastback with a 1500cc engine is exhibited in the Technical Museum in Brno, Moravia, and there are unconfirmed reports of more survivors, including another 1500 estate. I have also recently read that there is another 1500 saloon in the Museum of Transport, Bratislava, Slovakia, and to my understanding, this car is waiting to be restored.

The Octavia story is now drawing to its end. The greatness of this entirely indigenous Czechoslovakian design and product is in the fact that the Octavia was designed and built under difficult circumstances prevailing in a Communist-ruled country. It was not perfect, but it was one of the best small family cars in the late 1950s and early 1960s. The poor planning and permanent underfunding associated with the directive economy resulted in the Octavia being outclassed by much more modern rivals from 1963 onwards. The 720 would have been too late to prevent this, but the position could have been reversed a few years later. Admittedly, the entry-level Škoda 720-1250 would probably have been somewhat underpowered, but the bigger-engined models would have held their own just as well as the Octavia did against its competitors of the same generation.

# EPILOGUE

## Dear readers,

**THANK YOU** for taking the time to read this book. I hope you have enjoyed reading about old Škodas and their (mostly) capable creators from my old country. The Octavia is close to my heart as it was my parents' first car. When I drive my Old Girl, childhood memories come flooding back. However, the main reason I consider it a great car is the Octavia's success against daunting odds.

Another interesting aspect of the Octavia, and indeed of many classic cars is their small size; the Octavia is slightly larger than some of its British equivalents such as the Morris Minor, but still very small. With the notable exception of the French Panhard PL17, any small family car of the early 1960s was barely the size of a modern supermini.

Having done more research and found more accurate details, I have amended some statements I had made in *Cars from my Old Country*. This is in connection with the Spartak and Octavia but also Škoda 720. For details, please see the Amendments, listed after the Glossary.

I freely admit that I felt a tinge of sadness on more than one occasion when writing this book. So much ability and creative potential of Czechoslovakian designers, engineers and workers had been wasted by the authoritarian regime! The success of the Octavia was most certainly not achieved under the leadership of the Communist Party, but like many other Czechoslovakian successes, it was achieved in spite of the party's inept interventions.

I hope that you have found some of my personal memories amusing. I apologise for my digressions describing the features and actions of the Communist regime and, hopefully, reading about many similarities between the extreme Stalinist form of Communism and the Nazi regime has not made you feel too uncomfortable. I became even more acutely aware of them when doing research for *Cars from my Old Country* as well as for this book. Sadly, people with authoritarian tendencies can be found in any nation, and no country, regardless of how democratic, is immune. It all seems to be about their way of thinking: they believe it is okay to harm other people in the name of some (usually absurd) ideology. Few of today's 'Communists' refer to themselves as such, but they have all the hatred, bigotry, incompetence and above all, dishonesty.

Hopefully, those short digressions might be helpful by offering some insight into the wider historic, political and economic context in which the cars of the Octavia family were designed and built.

**ALL THE BEST**
**MIROSLAV ('MIREK') SYNEK**

# GLOSSARY

**2+2** Cabin accommodation with two full-size front seats and two small rear seats. The rear seats are often for children or, if necessary, for adults on short journeys.

**ABS** Short for Anti-lock Braking System. ABS is a safety anti-skid braking system where the wheels are prevented from locking up during hard braking. The wheels retain traction which significantly increases the driver's control over the vehicle. Modern computerised systems emerged in the early 1970s.

**Air conditioning** Also known as air-con, this is a device taking heat away from the air and regulating humidity in an enclosed space. The system operates on the basis of vapour compression using the forced circulation and phase change of a refrigerant from gas to liquid and back to transfer heat. Developing a unit sufficiently compact to be installed in a car took a long time. Much progress in this area was made in the pre-WW2 US, where Packard cars were the first to have air conditioning fitted from 1939.

**Alternator** Small generator converting the engine's mechanical energy into an electrical current. The electricity then charges the battery and powers ancillary equipment such as lights, wiper motors etc. The alternator produces an alternating current and is more efficient than a dynamo which produces a direct current (in the same direction). Alternators gradually replaced dynamos in the 1960s-1970s.

**Beam-type axle** An axle consisting of a single beam with a wheel on each end, suspended by leaf or coil springs. Beam axles front and rear was a typical layout in the 1920s and much of the 1930s. Technically more advanced cars started using independent suspension (either at the front only or at the front and rear) from the mid-1930s onwards.

**Bhp** This stands for brake horsepower and refers to a measurement of power output of an engine. Bhp is measured by applying a special 'brake' to the crankshaft on an engine test bed. This makes it possible to account for frictional losses in power. Power is calculated from torque multiplied by engine rpm. Brake horsepower is always a little less than engine horsepower (horsepower minus what it takes to run the engine).

**Bore** The diameter of the engine's cylinder(s).

**Cabriolet** Typically, a two-door car with a folding or removable fabric roof. Unlike roadsters, cabriolets are usually not sports cars.

**Camshaft** Rotating shaft with lobes that open and close the inlet and exhaust valves. It can operate the valves directly in an OHC (Overhead Camshaft) engine or indirectly in an OHV (Overhead Valve) engine. The indirect operation is typically by pushrods.

**CC** Short for cubic centimetres, the standard measurement of the volume (or capacity) of an engine's cylinders as swept by the pistons. The engine capacity is often given in cu in (cubic inches) in the US.

**Central tube chassis** Design of chassis (see below) with a central tube and perpendicular cross members. The body is attached to the cross members.

**Chassis** Originally a French word describing a load-bearing frame on wheels to which the body is attached. The frame is normally made of steel, but some cars in the early 1920s and beyond had a wooden chassis. Modern cars are of unitary construction (also known as monocoque – see below) and do not have a separate chassis. However, the term survives and now refers to the drivetrain assembly.

**Communist Party of Czechoslovakia** The authoritarian supposedly left-wing Communist Party was in power in Czechoslovakia from 1948 to 1989. It was toppled by non-violent mass protests involving the vast majority of Czechoslovakians (The Velvet Revolution). The party was declaring its support for social justice, equal opportunities, reduction of inequalities and removal of exploitation. This made sense and initially gained the party a good deal of popular support. Unfortunately, the real policies were completely different, indeed often the opposite. As a result, Communism soon came to be perceived as one big scam. The lack of freedom, intolerance of alternative views and general disrespect for individuals were other typical features.

In fairness, the Communist regime did put in place some positive social measures such as universal free health care (in fact pre-war Czechoslovakia already had an advanced system of universal health insurance) and free higher education. Both health care and education were of generally good standard in spite of the party's interference. However, there was always a huge discrepancy between the party's manifestos and actions. This dishonesty totally discredited the party over the years and ultimately led to its downfall.

I should emphasise that by no means all individual Communists were ideological maniacs or crooks. A number of thoroughly decent people joined the party in the late 1940s when they believed in its declared (but not acted on) programme. In later years, many people did so to be able to do their job properly as party membership was a precondition for a number of highly qualified jobs. There were even misguided individuals joining the party in good faith and hoping that they could influence its policies to become more socially responsible and patriotic. Those members soon realised that decent people did not stand much chance in the higher party circles.

**Compression ratio** The compression ratio is the ratio of maximum to minimum volume during the compression stage of the power cycle in a piston engine. Raising compression ratio enables an engine to produce more power, but is more demanding both of materials of construction and quality of fuel.

**Connecting rod** Also known as con-rod, this connects the piston with the crankshaft. Its role is to convert the reciprocating (up and down) movement of the pistons into rotation.

**Convertible** More common synonym for cabriolet (see earlier). However, some convertibles have a detachable hard top.

**Coefficient of drag** Also known as drag coefficient, this is the result of a complex scientific calculation referring to the resistance of the body to airflow. The calculation was based on using wind tunnels from the mid-1930s onwards, and the term is normally shortened to Cd and given to two decimal places. As a rule of thumb, the lower the Cd the more aerodynamic the car. The 1948 Tatraplan with Cd of 0.32 was way ahead of its time and would compare favourably with many cars until quite recently.

**Coupé** Originally a French word literally meaning cut. This refers to a two-door, usually sporting car with a low (cut down) roof line.

**Crankshaft** The main engine shaft that

converts the reciprocating (up and down) movement of the pistons into a rotary movement to turn the wheels.

**Cylinder** The cylindrical cavity in which the pistons move up and down.

**Cylinder block** The body of cast iron or (in later cars) aluminium into which cylinders are bored to carry pistons.

**Cylinder head** The upper part of the engine attached to the top of the cylinder block. The head (often used shorthand) contains the spark plugs and usually the valves.

**Czechoslovakian** Referring to or originating from Czechoslovakia, the country in Central Europe existing in 1918-1993 when it was partitioned into the Czech Republic and the Slovak Republic by the decision of its politicians. There was no referendum as the politicians (Czech and Slovak alike) were well aware that the vast majority of Czechs and Slovaks were opposed to the country's partition. A person of Czechoslovakian origin could be a Czech, a Slovak or possibly a member of another ethnic group living within the territory of Czechoslovakia. Analogically, a Briton could originate from England, Wales, Scotland or Northern Ireland.

**Differential** A gear-set in the drive system of a car that allows the outer wheel to rotate faster than the inner wheel. This is very important when turning corners. Many cars up to the mid-1930s did not have a differential. This simplified production and maintenance, but worsened handling and roadholding.

**Disc brakes** A braking system where each wheel hub contains a disc rotating with the wheel. If the car needs to be stopped, the disc is gripped by the brake pads. Disc brakes were introduced to many cars in the 1970s, initially in front. Disc brakes all round have become common from the 1990s onwards. The main advantage compared to drum brakes is higher efficiency.

**Distributor** A device transferring high voltage from the ignition coil to the spark plugs in the right firing order.

**Double de-clutching** A traditional method of changing gears in vehicles with unsynchronised gearboxes to match the speed of gears to be meshed. The gear change has two phases: 1 depressing the clutch pedal, selecting neutral and releasing the clutch pedal, then 2 depressing the clutch pedal again, selecting the required gear and releasing the clutch. The throttle needs to be blipped while the gearbox is in neutral when changing down, to achieve better meshing. This method is now used in many classic cars but also certain lorries.

**Driveshaft** Revolving shaft(s) transferring power from the final drive to the wheels.

**Drivetrain** The term covers mechanical parts of the car, such as the engine, gearbox, driveshaft(s) and differential.

**Drum brakes** A braking system with drums attached to the car's wheels; the brake shoes are pressed against the inner surface of the drum.

**Dynamo** An engine-driven generator of electric power in the form of direct current, now long replaced by the alternator (see also Alternator). The main weakness of the dynamo is that it needs an expensive commutator and carbon brushes which wear out and have to be replaced regularly.

**Entry-level** The car with the lowest specification (and usually lowest price) in the range.

**Estate** A car with a loading area in the rear. The loading area is typically larger than in a hatchback and accessible via a tailgate or, rarely, twin-hinged door. The Czech equivalent is Kombi or Combi (both spellings acceptable).

**Fastback** A car with roof line sloping towards

the rear. There is normally a boot lid but not a tailgate.

**Flat-twin, flat-four engine** This layout is characterised by cylinders positioned in two horizontally opposed banks serving a single crankshaft. These engines are sometimes called 'boxer' engines as the pistons in opposing cylinders are moving towards and away from each other like boxers throwing punches.

**Four-stroke engine** An internal combustion engine where the power cycle consists of four stages with two crankshaft rotations: intake, compression, power and exhaust. Each of these is associated with upward or downward movements of the piston(s). The four-stroke design is now universal in cars.

**Front-wheel drive** A design where power is transmitted to the front wheels, the most common layout at present. The advantage is weight saving as there is no need for a transmission shaft to the rear wheels. Potential disadvantage can be understeer at higher cornering speeds.

**Fuel injection** A fuel supply system that replaced the carburettor. The fuel is sprayed by the injectors into the inlet ports where it mixes with air before being ignited in the cylinders. The fuel is injected straight into the cylinders in diesel and direct-injection petrol engines. Fuel injection was slowly introduced from the 1960s onwards and now is universal in modern cars.

**Hard top** A car with a rigid roof, fixed or removable.

**Hatchback** A car with a large door at the sloping back opening upwards. The door is usually referred to as a tailgate. This layout increases versatility compared to saloon cars, but the load area is smaller than in a comparable estate.

**Hydraulic brakes** A braking system using fluid to transfer pressure from the brake pedal to the braking mechanism (brake shoes or calipers). Hydraulic brakes were gradually introduced from the 1930s onwards and have long become standard. They are much more efficient than mechanical brakes.

**Independent suspension** A suspension system allowing each wheel to move up and down independently of the others. The main advantages are better handling and a more comfortable ride compared to cars with beam-type axles.

**km/h (or kph)** Short for kilometres per hour, the metric speed unit used in continental Europe and elsewhere. The ratio to miles per hour (mph) is 1 mile=1.609km.

**Leaf spring** Also known as a cart spring, this is a traditional means of suspension consisting of overlaid arcs (leaves) of steel fixed to the underside of the car. This forms a shock-absorbing cushion on which the car's axle presses. There are various sub-types such as elliptical, semi-elliptical or even quarter-elliptical leaf springs, differing in shape. Leaf springs can be longitudinal or transverse. They are noted for their durability, but do not provide much in the way of ride comfort.

**Live axle** Typically, a beam-type axle through which power is transmitted to the wheels.

**MacPherson strut suspension** Named after its inventor Earl MacPherson, this consists of a hydraulic shock absorber with a co-axial coil spring. MacPherson suspension is typically used in front and minimises the intrusion into the engine bay.

**McCarthyism** Named after US Senator Joseph McCarthy, its main promoter, this is a practice of making spurious accusations of treason or lack of patriotism. This campaign in the US reached its peak in the late 1940s and early 1950s. Many American intellectuals and public figures were (mostly falsely) accused of being Communists, sacked from their jobs and blacklisted for a variety of employments. The investigations were carried out by the House Committee on Un-American activities, a newly established branch of the US Congress. McCarthyism was discredited by 1954, but caused lasting damage to US society. Several thousand people were affected (the figures are not clear, but probably below 10,000). The purges in post-1968 Czechoslovakia affected most likely in excess of half a million. It should be mentioned that Czechoslovakia had a very small fraction (c7%) of the US population, therefore the impact was incomparably greater.

**Monocoque** Car body of unitary construction, ie without a separate chassis.

**OHC** Overhead Camshaft, an engine layout with the camshaft in the cylinder head driven by bevel gears, chain, or, more recently, by toothed belt. An overhead camshaft reduces the inertia of the valve operation mechanism, principally by eliminating the camshaft followers and pushrods of an overhead valve engine.

**OHV** Overhead Valve, an engine layout with the valves in the cylinder head operated indirectly, typically via pushrods.

**Overdrive** Effectively an additional gearbox attached to the main unit and activated mechanically or electrically. Overdrive makes possible more relaxed cruising at higher speeds and lower engine rpm.

**Over-square engine** An engine with the cylinder bore greater than the stroke.

**Piston** The engine component moving up and down inside the cylinder. It transfers force from the expanding gas to the crankshaft on the combustion stroke.

**Piston ring** An open-ended ring fitted to a groove on the outer surface of an engine's piston. Its purpose is to seal the combustion chamber, also to cool the piston by transferring heat to the cylinder wall. If piston rings are worn, oil consumption rises. Blue smoke is the typical sign. There are typically three piston rings in a four-stroke engine. The top two are 'compression rings' principally for sealing purposes, the lower one is the 'oil-control ring' principally for scraping oil from the cylinder walls back into the crankcase.

**Powertrain** Another expression for drivetrain (see earlier).

**Q-car** A powerful, high-performance car of ordinary appearance. The name is derived from Q-ships used by the Royal Navy in WW1 mainly against enemy submarines. Q-ships were of harmless appearance but heavily armed and well-protected.

**Rack-and-pinion steering** This consists of two gears converting rotational motion into linear motion. It is now an almost universal system of car steering. The main advantages are good accuracy and feedback to the driver. It is also easier and cheaper to power-assist than a steering box.

**Radiator** A heat exchanger that cools liquids (coolants) by presenting a large surface to airflow. If it is silted up, cooling efficiency drops dramatically. On a car the radiator is generally placed at the front and usually derives sufficient airflow from forward motion.

**Rallye Monte-Carlo (or Monte Carlo Rally)** Traditional motor race running from 1911 to this day. Originally, it started in various points in Europe at the same distance (634 miles or 1020km) from Monte Carlo and converged on Monte Carlo. The event now takes place only along the French Riviera, with the finish remaining in Monte Carlo.

**Roadster** A light two-door sports car usually of small size with two seats and foldable fabric roof. Some roadsters feature the 2+2 layout. Traditionally, the doors had cut-outs for elbows, but this practice was largely abandoned by the end of the 1950s.

A few roadsters had a bench seat for three passengers sitting abreast, but such an arrangement was rare.

**Rpm or r/min** Short for revolutions per minute and referring to one turn of the crankshaft as a measure of engine speed. A high-revving engine does many revolutions per minute, the opposite is a low-revving engine.

**Running board** A fixed step or ledge below the doors making entry and exit easier. This was helpful in cars with high ground clearance as they were built up to the early 1930s. Running boards started to disappear from the mid-1930s onwards as cars were built with lower ground clearance.

**Saloon** A car with a fixed metal roof, two- or four-door. Interestingly, the American expression 'sedan' rather than 'saloon' was used in Czechoslovakia.

**Screw-and-nut steering** Steering system with a screw (aka worm) moving against the nut in a steering box. Compared to rack-and pinion steering, it is less accurate.

**Semi-trailing arm suspension** An independent suspension assembly for the rear wheels where each wheel hub is linked to the chassis by the lower triangular arm which pivots at an acute angle to the centre-line of the car.

**Servo-assisted brakes** The vacuum servo, also known as a brake booster, is a device assisting the driver by reducing the effort necessary for effective braking.

**Sill** The section of bodywork between the front and rear wheelarches and below the doors. Sills are structural in monocoque cars, non-structural in cars with a separate chassis.

**Sodomka coachbuilders** Probably the most famous coachbuilders in pre-war Czechoslovakia, the company was founded by Mr Josef Sodomka in 1896 to build carriages. The founder's son, Josef Sodomka Jnr instigated the building of car bodies in 1925. This started a highly successful era which produced some brilliant designs. Many indigenous as well as foreign cars were fitted with custom-built Sodomka bodies, particularly in the 1930s. One of their products was the body for a La Salle car ordered by the British Royal Family in 1938. More about this story is in *Cars from my Old Country*. The company was nationalized in 1948, but Mr Sodomka was allowed to remain as a Managing Director. Unfortunately, this sensible arrangement did not last long. Mr Sodomka was arrested on totally spurious charges in 1950 and spent three years in prison. After release he was not allowed to return and the company was re-named Karosa.

**SV** Side Valve. An engine layout with valves on the side of the cylinders rather than in the cylinder head. The side valves are typically on the same side of the cylinders. Some SV engines use the T-head or cross-flow layout with the intake and exhaust valves on the opposite sides of the cylinders. SV engines were used in some Czechoslovakian (and other European) cars until the end of the 1930s. Their advantages include simplicity, reliability and low manufacturing costs. The main disadvantage is less efficient combustion due to the sideways position of the combustion chamber. This results in low power output and high emissions.

**Straight engine (straight-four, straight-six etc)** An engine with cylinders in line. Another expression is in-line engine.

**Supermini** One of the main classes of cars, describing a small hatchback, traditionally with a four-cylinder engine but recently often with a three-cylinder.

**Suspension** A system protecting the structure and occupants of a car from excessive movements of the wheels as they ride over rough and uneven surfaces.

**Synchromesh gearbox** A gearbox with synchromesh (also known as synchroniser rings). The rings automatically match the speed of the input shaft with that of the gear selected, which removes the need for matching these speeds manually, typically by double-de-clutching. Fully synchromesh gearboxes have been universal since the mid to late 1960s.

**Torque** The turning effort produced by the engine. It is measured in lb/ft (pounds per foot) in the UK and Nm (Newton metres) in continental Europe. The conversion rate is 1lb/ft=1.36 Nm (approximately).

**Torsion bar** A rod or tube of tempered steel as part of a suspension system acting as a spring when twisted by movements of the wheels.

**Track** The distance between the wheels on the same axle (also referred to as wheel track).

**Trafficator** A direction indicator device consisting of a semaphore arm with a small light. When activated, the arm protruded from the side of the car and showed which way the driver intended to turn. Trafficators were gradually replaced by far more effective (and therefore safer) flashing indicator lights permanently visible on the bodywork from the mid-1930s onwards. They were becoming progressively less common after WW2 and disappeared from new cars by the early 1950s.

**Turning circle** The diameter of the circle described by the outer front wheel when the car is turning with its steering at full lock.

**Two-stroke engine** An internal combustion engine where the power cycle consists of only two strokes (up and down movements of the pistons) rather than four as in a four-stroke engine (see above). In a two-stroke engine the end of combustion and beginning of compression take place at the same time. The intake and exhaust cycles also happen simultaneously. The advantage of two-stroke engines is simplicity due to fewer moving parts. They are often light which gives them a good power-to-weight ratio. The main disadvantage is high emissions due to lubrication by oil added to fuel in various ratios, typically around 1:30. Two-stroke cars were notorious for producing huge amounts of blue-greyish, smelly smoke. This was becoming more of a problem from the 1960s, and high emissions were the main reason why production of two-stroke car engines was terminated by about 1990. Another disadvantage is less effective combustion resulting in higher fuel consumption compared to a four-stroke engine of the same size.

**Unitary construction** Another expression for monocoque body.

**Wheelbase** The distance between the front and rear axle.

## AMENDMENTS

**I STATED** in my previous book, *Cars from my Old Country* that the Škoda Spartak and Octavia had a light alloy cylinder head. This is inaccurate: further research confirmed that they had a light alloy block and cast-iron cylinder head.

Another error in *Cars from my Old Country* concerns the Škoda 720. The larger 1771cc engine was in fact installed in at least one prototype, successfully tested and probably fitted to one of the fastback prototypes. Please accept my apologies.

# REFERENCES


### Books

Cedrych MR, Nachtmann L: *Škoda-auta známá i neznámá* (*Škoda - the cars known and unknown*). Grada Publishing, Prague 2007

Chapman G: *Cars we Loved in the 1950s.* The History Press, Stroud, Gloucestershire 2015

Chapman G, Gurdon M, Long D, Noakes A, Quiller-Rees C: *The Classic Car Book.* Dorling Kindersley, London 2016

Gereg J: *Od Spartaka k Octavii 1953-1971* (*From Spartak to Octavia 1953-1971*). Technical Publishing House, Hradec Králové 2004

Hausman J, Kovářík M: *Vteřiny za volantem* (*Seconds behind the steering wheel*). Nakladatelství Dopravy a Spojů (Transport and Communications Publishing House), Prague 1968

Noakes A: *The Classic Car Book.* Haynes Publishing, Sparkford, Somerset 2006

Novill J: *East European Cars.* Sutton Publishing Ltd, Stroud, Gloucestershire 2000

Šuman-Hreblay M: *Dvě století českých automobilů* (*Two centuries of Czech cars). C press*, Albatros Media Group, Prague 2015

Tuček J: *Spartak, Octavia, Felicia.* Grada Publishing Prague 2010

Tuček J: *Škoda-Zapomenuté vozy 1960-1990* (*Škoda-Forgotten Cars 1960-1990*). Grada Publishing, Prague, 2007

### Periodicals

*Auto Tip Klassik.* Czech News Center, Prague, 2017-2023

*Classic Car Weekly.* Bauer Media Group 2017-2023

*Practical Classics.* H Bauer Publishing Ltd, 2017-2023

### Websites

www.auta5p.eu

www.auto.cz

www.autobible.euro.cz

www.autoforum.cz

www.auto-mania.cz

www.autorevue.cz

www.eurooldtimers.cz

www.rajveteranu.cz (ráj veteránů as spelt correctly in Czech means paradise of classics)

www.wikipedia.com

www.ceskatelevize.cz/porady/10209988352-zaslapane-projekty/

*Zašlapané Projekty* was a Czech TV series. It means 'Projects trampled into the ground' and describes advanced projects from Czechoslovakian designers banned or killed off by the Communist Party.

# INDEX